Goose River Anthology, 2017

Edited by

Deborah J. Benner

Goose River Press
Waldoboro, Maine

Copyright © 2017 Goose River Press

All rights reserved. No part of this book may be reproduced in any form without written permission from the publisher, except by a reviewer who may quote brief passages in a review to be printed in a newspaper or magazine.

Library of Congress Card Number: 2017913954

ISBN: 978-1-59713-180-3

First Printing, 2017

Cover photo by Deborah J. Benner

Published by
Goose River Press
3400 Friendship Road
Waldoboro ME 04572
e-mail: gooseriverpress@roadrunner.com
www.gooseriverpress.com

Authors Included

Ackermann, Helen: Pages 99, 220, 235
Altieri, Carol Leavitt: Pages 82, 246-247
Andersen, Judith: Pages 67-68
Archer, Lloyd: Pages 5-8
Augusta: Pages 31-32
Babcock, Janice: Pages 1-2
Barsalou, Edward O.: Pages 50, 146
Belenardo, Sally: Pages 12, 220
Bennett, Thomas Peter: Pages 3, 54, 211
Biehl, Mark D.: Pages 63, 178-179, 195
Bloom, Stephen: Pages 199-205
Brown, Peggy F.: Pages 227-231
Bruno, Donna: Pages 196-197
Buck, Lilli: Pages 170-172
Campbell, David: Pages 218-219
Charbonneau, Paul G.: 35, 123, 214, 238
Clements, Jennifer: Pages 73-81
Coleman, Diana: Pages 189-194
Collins, Java L.: Pages 236-238
Conlon, Sandy: Pages 66, 143, 213
Crowley, Tom: Pages 86, 184, 247-248
D'Alessandro, F. Anthony: Pages 10-11, 234
Dailey, Genie: Page 16
Driscoll, John P.: Pages 249-257
Erickson, Robert: Page 122
Fahy, Christopher: Pages 30, 125, 160, 258
Ferriss, Lloyd: Pages 119-121
Fiori, Manny: Pages 52, 198
George, Gerald: Pages 108-110
Gillis, Christina Marsden: Pages 57-61
Goldfinger, Stephen.: Pages 215-216
Gray, Joe: Page 126

Authors Included

Haben, OSF, Laureen: Pages 64, 224-225
Hagan, John T.: Pages 137-140
Hanson, Sherry Ballou: Page 100
Harrington, Ilga Winicov: Pages 37-46
Hedou, Joanne: Pages 239-240
Hildebrandt, Leonore: Pages 17, 107
Janover, Caroline: Pages 173-175
Johnson, Frank S.: Pages 241-245
Knuckles, Jeffry: Pages 152-154
Lawrence, Jean: Pages 9, 208
Leddin, Taylor: Page 180
L'Heureux, Juliana: Pages 155-157
Lie-Nielsen, Karyn: Pages 72, 169
Lincoln, Sidney Cowles: Pages 13-15
Little-Sweat, Sylvia: Pages 17, 95, 118, 124-125, 136, 160, 197, 206-207, 208, 217
Manichello, Richard: Pages 127-131
Mariotti, Celine Rose: Page 147-149
Mason, Mary Jane: Pages 51-52
Maurice, Camille Wade: Page 83
McFarland, Paul: Pages 144-145
McHugh, Kathy: Pages 181-184
Millick, Kim: Pages 101-107
Moorehead, P. C.: Pages 15, 65, 85, 142, 180, 226
Moreland, Robert B.: Pages: 18, 50, 71, 132, 161
Morgan, Janet: Pages 211-223
Munson, Sharon Lask: Pages 46, 117, 207
Nesset, Miriam: Pages 163-168
O'Kane, John: Pages 87-95
Onion, Pat: Page 118
Parker, T. Blen: Pages 55-56
Passineau, Elmae: Pages 110, 158-159

Authors Included

Radoff, Phillip L.: Pages 19-27
Randolph, Patrick T.: Pages 98, 188, 194, 205
Reitz, Diane C.: Page 62
Rice, Julia: Pages 69, 172, 219, 233
Rickards, Laura: Page 53
Roncone, Margaret: Page 33, 154, 223
Schmitz, Art: Page 195
Schmoll, Edie: Pages 142, 179
Seguin, Marilyn Weymouth: Pages 111-113
Sipe, Craig: Pages 212-213
Stewart, Roselyn: Pages 141, 176, 185
Stires, A. McKinne: Pages 16, 114-115, 133, 151
Stout, Deb: Pages 48-49
Taylor, Ellen M.: Pages 47, 177
Taylor, Richard: Pages 49, 162
Timmerman, Jacinda: Pages 28-30, 84-85
Trojan, Peggy: Pages 36, 97, 175
Troyanovich, Steve: Pages 4, 116, 150, 231
Von Rosenberg, Byron: Pages 96-97
Wagner, Karen: Pages 34-35, 136, 232-233
Weiss, Dorothy M.: Pages 209-211
Wells-Meyer, Trudy: Pages 186-188
Winters, Rena & Corbin, Ron: Pages 70-71
Witte, Robert: Page 64
Zimmerman, Irene: Pages 27, 113, 134-135

*Dedicated to
Cora Jean Benner*

and in memory of

*Edward O. Barsalou
Joe Gray*

Goose River Anthology, 2017

Janice Babcock
Wauwatosa, WI

My Gaucho

It was the day of my gaucho trip in Argentina cowboy country. I entered the pampas, a very flat almost treeless grassland. About 70 miles from Buenos Aires. We were now in real cattle country.

I entered the elegant wrought iron gate to the ranch which encompassed just under 3,000 acres. We were welcomed with refreshments and traditional empanadas. I mingled with the crowd. The younger gauchos wore tam-like caps and had no mustaches. My gaucho immediately stood out.

He had a gray-black mustache, leathered skin and black kerchief around his neck. My gaucho wore a black Zorro style hat with a flat crown, a brim and corded chin strap. He wore traditional gaucho baggy trousers, both pants and shirt were white. His broad leather belt provided support to his back for long hours in the saddle. The thick belt was an important part of his garb. It was decorated with rows of shiny coins and silver chains.

He had tall black leather boots with spurs to encourage his horse. A gaucho without his horse is like a man without his legs. He looked distinguished, a true Argentine icon.

My first exposure to my amazing gaucho was when I rode in his horse-drawn carriage. It was tricky to climb up a single, metal foot print-size step on the back of what reminded me of a Western buck-board. It was not an elegant carriage like I expected. It was pulled by two large horses. The rugged wood and metal wheels supported a large wood box holding twelve of us. It was a rough ride on the pampas. I balanced myself between the other riders. The surrounding foliage was different, leaving an exotic aroma in the air. My gaucho manipulated this vintage horse drawn carriage with finesse and majesty.

Janice Babcock
Wauwatosa, WI

After the carriage ride, again, my gaucho performed an equestrian elite dance when gathering about a dozen of his horses, kicking up clouds of dust. This showman bowed to the right and left to introduce his horses. I admired his spirited horsemanship. Gauchos have an air of independence, bravery, and honor. Mine certainly did.

After an Argentine feast of exceptional beef and drink in a Spanish style barbecue and folk entertainment, we adjourned to the rodeo area. Gauchos challenged each other's horseback riding skills. Each rode full tilt to race and grab at the traditional ribbon on a high wire. The winner presented his prize to a senorita. In turn she gave him a kiss.

Next, I was completely taken by surprise. My travel mates encouraged me to join my gaucho, to ride double with him. I blurted out, "No, no I had something to drink! I cannot fall off his horse and break my leg just before tonight's flight home."

My group shouted louder, "Just get on the horse!" I froze. In spite of the danger, a ride with an authentic gaucho could be thrilling. My time had arrived! I would take that once in a lifetime risk!

I climbed on a platform and mounted the horse with my gaucho. I had no stirrups for my feet. I had no bridle to hold on to. I had no saddle to sit on, only part of his blanket. I clung on to my gaucho as best I could. We took off galloping around the ranch. His horse's hooves thundered as we rode quite a distance. It was a dusty, but exhilarating ride. Blue skies with fluffy clouds formed our backdrop.

My gaucho spoke no English, I spoke no Spanish. However, between my body language and laughter, I'm sure he knew my feelings. I felt safe with him and was having fun.

I gave my handsome gaucho a kiss. He looked deep into my eyes and smiled. Then, I gave him two more kisses with a big hug. What a memory from South America.

Olé!

Thomas Peter Bennett
Silver Springs, MD

Changing Seasons

After fifty years of blissful upsizing,
    A decade of equalizing, and minor trimming—
Now, agonizing, wrenching, downsizing,
    Saying goodbye to piano, books, paintings
For our encore retirement move.

The Steinway, a family wedding gift,
    Hoisted through the window of our
Third-floor walkup apartment, for
    Mozart to warm our home.

Audubon, Faulkner, Whitman...
    Texts, monographs, dictionaries...
Collections of art, history, nature...
    Abandoned, stored now in Kindle or in clouds.

Paintings sorted, measured, accessed for
    Future hangings or storage, donated to museums...
Silver, china, crystal: no family member interest...
    Photo albums and pictures in boxes tossed after
Scanning, cloud and CD archiving.

Our new apartment awaits us
    Seven hundred miles away,
Near our son's and daughter's homes.
Like our immigrant forebears,
    We face a new world
To bloom where we are planted.

First published in *Encore Seasons* by **Goose River Press**, 2017.

Steve Troyanovich
Florence, NJ

the longing to love
for Elizabeth

> *el ansia de amar*
> *entra en tu boca*
> *y yo con ella*
> —Alberto Ruy Sanchez

the touch
of your lips
holds tomorrow's
promise…

in your mouth
the sun rises
a flower
burning my hands…

holding the wind
i caress
the skin of the world
covering you…

Lloyd Archer
Mapleton, ME

Spring Mountain

It was her idea, what could he do? He was the one that said he wanted her to think of something for them to do together. He always came up with the idea; she went along. Sometimes he wondered if she would ever say no to anything. She always had a good time but he always wondered why she never thought of anything on her own. Finally, he refused to do anything until she thought of a weekend activity for them.

Now he was having second thoughts. Not because of the activity, it was her attitude. It was as if forcing her to pick something had broken some unwritten rule and this was her way of showing him she did not like to choose. Since they started the trip, she was not her usual self. She answered his questions with short answers, volunteered no conversation and made no eye contact. They got off the plane and picked up the rental car almost without speaking and not a word since. He never saw her go this long without a smile, let alone laughing.

The mountains surrounded them now. At about 10,000 feet, they started seeing patches of snow in the ditch and under trees. The old pickup truck they rented had good tires, was running fine and didn't seem to be using much gas, if he could trust the gauge. The owner told him there were tire chains behind the seat and recommended he use them. "Don't wait until you're stuck to put them on," he said. "You might not have time then."

Jerry asked him what he meant by that.

With a concerned look the man said, "Just do as I tell you and hope you don't find out."

The road had a flat stretch so he decided he would use it and put them on now. The chains were in two canvas bags, a pair in each bag, with two bungee cords thrown in on top of each pair. He stretched the chains out in front of each of

Lloyd Archer
Mapleton, ME

the tires, taking his time to keep them flat with no twists in the crosslinks, then got in and drove ahead until the tires were in the center of the chains. He pulled each end up on top of the tire until they met and got them as tight as he could and hooked the connectors, then put the bungee cords on to take up the little slack left. He got back in and drove a half mile to a turnout, where he tightened them again. He saw a car, years ago, that was driven with loose chains; the fenders were trashed. The ride was noisier because of the chains but it wasn't as if it was interfering with any conversation.

The snow covered the ground now everywhere but the road, where it had melted. When they came out on a plateau where the sign read elevation 12,307 ft., he pulled over and she got out, pulling her parka on as she walked. He watched her for a moment before getting out. The sun glistened off the snow and he was glad for his sunglasses.

She walked to the edge of the small parking area and stood looking out over the vista, hood up, hands in the pockets of her coat. She seemed to shrink somehow, maybe it was his imagination, but her shoulders drooped and even from this distance, he sensed a sadness. He had no idea why. They had been together for three years now. He knew of nothing in her past that gave him any insight into her behavior.

He got out and walked over near where she was standing, available but not intruding. The wind was cold; he pulled his hood up and waited. Fifteen minutes passed without either of them moving before she turned and walked by him back to the truck without acknowledging his presence. He followed, got in the truck, and waited. She looked out the side window for ten minutes. She said when she picked this trip she wanted to go to the top; he started the truck and drove on. She made no response.

He went along slowly, driving in snow now, the road still distinguishable because it was the only flat surface. Near the

Lloyd Archer
Mapleton, ME

peak, they reached a round flat area, the end of the road, elevation 14,230 ft. The snow was about a foot deep. She got out again, this time walking up to the peak, standing again, her sadness palpable from the truck. He waited. This was her thing; he would respect her space. He certainly didn't understand it but didn't need to. She wanted to come here; she must have a reason. They laughed at how they seemed to know what each other was thinking most of the time but not today. He got the sadness, he could feel it but had no inkling of the reason for it and he certainly couldn't read her thoughts. She stood there in the cold wind until he started to worry about her. The coat was warm but she was wearing light shoes and slacks.

Finally, he got out and walked up to where she stood, this time getting closer, putting his arm around her shoulder. She was a stranger; he felt no response from her at all. He looked down at her face and hardly recognized her. Her chin was set, her teeth clenched, eyes hollow. There were no tears but he had never seen so much sadness in a person's face, as if it was too deep for tears. He felt a force, almost physical, pushing him away.

He started to take his arm away but had a feeling if he did he would lose contact and never get it back. Squeezing her shoulders, he felt her soften slightly. He stepped around in front of her, blocking the view and held her in his arms. Slowly he felt her soften more and settle against his chest. He held her as she continued to rest against him more until he was supporting her. He turned her a little to her left and slid his right arm under her thighs, lifted her and carried her to the truck, head on his shoulder, as if she were unconscious. He let her down and she stood, his arm supporting her until he could open the door. He lifted her onto the seat and closed the door. She sat like a lump, staring straight ahead.

He started the truck, turned the heater up full blast and drove in low gear, even more thankful for the chains on the steep places than he had been on the way up. He watched

Lloyd Archer
Mapleton, ME

her as much as he could and stay in the road. She didn't move as he worked his way down the mountain to bare ground. When they got to the tarred road she stirred a little; he pulled over and removed the chains, throwing them in the back of the truck, planning to pack them away when he got back to where they rented it.

By the time they reached the garage she was looking around again, her eyes brighter; he felt the sadness easing. When he opened her door she looked at him as though she didn't recognize him for a second then turned to get out of the truck, nearly falling, catching the arm he extended to steady herself, leaning on it as he walked her to the rental car.

Jerry left her in the car and walked back toward the truck with plans to put the chains in the bags but the owner was there ahead of him, standing with his hands on his hips looking toward the car.

He said, "If I live to be a hundred I'll never understand it."

Jerry asked, "What's that?"

"Every spring some woman comes here and goes up that mountain. They usually die."

"Is that what you meant when you said to put the chains on before you get stuck, you might not have time when you are?"

The man looked at him. "That's what I meant. It looks like you listened. I'll put them away; you need to get her away from that mountain. Maybe we won't find a body this year."

Jean Lawrence
Waldoboro, ME

A Father's Love

I watched you take your first steps, hesitant and shaky.
I heard you speak words of joy in special moments.
As you grew, my heart regularly filled with pride.
Your youthful accomplishments showed such promise.

And then, the call of the world intervened.
Your demeanor changed; familial love no longer satisfied.
All we had shared no longer sufficed.
You demanded your share, turned, and left.

I grieved as step by step you walked away.
No longer did I hear you speak my name.
Home and my heart were lonely.
All the promises of growth, joy, and accomplishment were
 gone.

Life moved on; my responsibilities continued.
Your brother struggled with your choice and its impact.
He did not understand my grief at the hole you left in my
 heart.
No one could replace you.

And then bent, broken, and repentant, you appeared.
You knelt before me; you appealed for forgiveness.
My heart rejoiced at your return and request.
Old hurts were healed, and I welcomed you home.

This tale in other texts is called "The Prodigal Son."
The emphasis seems to be placed on the wayward child.
The misunderstanding of his brother touches and distracts
 us.
The true message: the everlasting love and welcome of the
 Father.

F. Anthony D'Alessandro
Celebration, FL

Our Captain's Classroom

A reluctant ocean cowpoke, scores of times I'd saddled that
swirling mound of ocean, framed by a flaking stone
    shouldered inlet.
Clutching the cabin's creaking handrail, I watched color
    desert my hands.
The trawler felt like a washer's spin dry cycle as it trudged
    thru rogue inlet waters.
Our swollen bronco boat halfheartedly protected its captain
    while he continually squeezed an
endless cup of muddy coffee and winked at his hall of fame
    collection of saints' holy cards pasted
around his cabin. All the while, he preached life lessons.
That mellow chief mariner made me feel safe throughout
my edgy Golf of Tonkin days, whenever I dared ride
in that squatty trawler thru Chief Shinnecock's back
    yard inlet.
The overmatched waddling fish boat rolled and rolled, clad
in a clumsy necklace of nets, a tangle of fishing door ear-
rings swaying and humming, all directed by the white-
    capped, old salt impresario.
That maritime raconteur provided a repertoire of tales for
every occasion, and eventually shared them with my sons
    too.
All that remains of that placid ancient mariner and his
parables on this side of the millennium are memories, and
my sons who were his sailor boys of summer, linked by
    genetics and surname.
Despite maritime bloodlines and family, as adults their
    links to the *Capitano's alto mare*
were severed and cast adrift. The young mariners shunned
    the siren call of the seas.
Sleepless nights haunt me as chilling inlet nightmares of
bobbing atop watery tidal walls of terror infect my dreams.

F. Anthony D'Alessandro
Celebration, FL

My boys, Twenty-First Century warriors, boast of pleasant
and cherished memories regarding inlet forays secured in
the scrapbooks of their minds. Negativity is banned by their
    reveries.
Despite my past bumpy cruises, worse than the scariest
coasters, when I thought Capitano's boat was about to
somersault me into a watery canyon, *Capitano* never
changed expression. He continued to weave his tales as if
we were by the fireplace in his home, rather than beside the
tarred, pot-bellied boat stove trembling more violently than
    a dirty floor mat beaten clean by my mom.
An abrasive ring shattered my teacher's afternoon slumber.
A shrill voice announced that the *Captaino*, a survivor of
the distant Pacific sea war, fell victim to a local Atlantic
    inlet wave.
That bullying sea sliced his tiny boat in much the same
    way as a karate master slashes wood.
Life vests, wisdom, and the guardian ships of the coast
plucked him from the frothing sea as the defenseless vessel
    slumped, then plunged toward the ocean floor.
That day, the *Capitano* accepted a brief rain check on life,
yet the crude caretaker of numbered days prevented his
    sailing the ocean again.
As I observe my boys, grown men now, dealing in dollars
Capitano never dreamed of, nor cared about, I hear of their
    repeating their ancient mariner's sound advice.
This wisdom filtered thru them from another time, another
    era, and another culture.
Capitano's sage suggestions support the stanchions of my
    sons' career successes on *terra firma*.
For my part, despite my terror-filled Atlantic Ocean days,
I'd risk one more sail, if possible just to hear *Capitano's* soft
spoken insights while directing his floating classroom.

Sally Belenardo
Branford, CT

Dragonfly's Visit

A whirring jewel skims lightning fast
across the lazy pond
and flies to me as though I'd waved
a wizard's magic wand.

At rest for merely seconds here,
her four transparent wings
refract the light in rainbow hues
while to my sleeve she clings.

I wear a weightless work of art,
a gem, enameled green,
more vivid than an emerald
or jade or tourmaline.

For years she dwelled a humble nymph,
the fish her predator,
then up a reed from water crawled,
shed skin, and fine wings bore.

A summer, only, lasts her life,
pursuing favorite fare
of thousands of mosquitoes caught
at full speed in the air.

So rare her flight to visit me
this warm September day,
that I will bid her bon voyage
before she darts away.

Sidney Cowles Lincoln
Falmouth, ME

Robert Strickland

One of the first things I did with my new LG G5 phone was to install Pandora and request Beethoven...to calm me while I tried to find the password for Wi-Fi...long forgotten ...and to pretend confidence in acquainting myself with this mini marvel.

And who should be playing but Robert Strickland...a soulful, soothing adagio. This cannot be my Robert Strickland...but could it? Robert, if you just had any idea of how much you have been with me for all these years.

Back in 1965, I was teaching first grade in Gloucester County, Guinea Neck, Achilles, Virginia. Guinea Neck is populated with fishing folk. Oysters, crabs, blue fish...

A good portion of my students were of parents with perhaps a second grade education who hid their money under the mattress, kept to themselves and if they were inclined to dress and go Sunday, attended the Baptist church next door to the elementary school. Both those imposing structures had been built entirely by the residents. There was among them: a fierce pride, independence, and self-sufficiency.

"This here's my boy Robert Strickland. Take good care of him."

Mrs. Strickland was a solid looking woman, a bit worn, wearing an obviously well-washed homemade dress.

Robert settled himself into the classroom with 34 other rather confused first graders. There was no kindergarten in those days.

I remember commenting on his jacket. A gray leather-looking jacket, a little soiled. He had hung it with such care. Who could not notice? "I got it from the dump," he said proudly.

Robert slid into the routine of taking his turn at groups, busying himself while doing seat work, and, I soon noticed,

Sidney Cowles Lincoln
Falmouth, ME

commandeering the others who might, just might, not have listened to the directions.

Because time is short, and because I need for you to know Robert Stickland in the manner of "what you do speaks so loud I cannot hear what you say," this is what he did.

My husband died. It was a traumatic event for the entire county. John was known, he was loved, he was revered, he was criticized, and the entire county attended his funeral. So Robert knew.

Robert Strickland stood beside me at recess and leaned into my knees. And just stayed there.

When I fell asleep during reading group (this can happen when you are a bit broken), I would wake and find Robert had kept the group in total order as they dutifully continued the story.

(Did I tell you Robert was selling fire balls at the bus stop for the exact amount of the cost of a lunch?)

And, amazingly, he made the Hansel a Gretel extravaganza...that!

I was taking credit hours at William and Mary. This particular semester I decided to add to my credits with an art course. We were to construct a poster...Can't remember the exact direction, but my vision was to create a visual for Hansel and Gretel. I acquired a refrigerator box, cut it into two sections of two, and presented to the class the question of what should be pictured...yes, the children in the woods, surely the parents...disappearing...and the stove flaming hot...but oh, the most fantastic...a picture of the witch's house...glorious, shining, alluring, tempting, enthralling... What shall we use for materials?

"Don't worry. I'll find the right stuff." That from Robert Strickland.

What he brought was a burlap bag of crushed glass. He had gathered, at the dump, red glass, blue glass, clear glass, green glass, into the bag then crushed all into tiny pieces.

Sidney Cowles Lincoln
Falmouth, ME

"Oh," we all said. "How perfect."
We glued and pasted all that glittering beauty to create the most magical witch's house.
Those images on the refrigerator boxes hung in the lunch room for all the years I was teaching there.
As I listen to Robert Strickland playing Beethoven, I look into People Search. There are Robert Stricklands whose bodies are not well tended. There are Robert Stricklands who look secure and successful. There are Robert Stricklands who look too used to see another day.
And then there is the...adagio.

***

P. C. Moorehead
North Lake, WI

Aging in Place

I am gnarled redwood.

Burl upon burl,
face darkening,
weathering storms,
I grow up and up.

Fresh bark, old bark,
new limbs, old limbs—
climbing the sky,
I break the night.

Old, new,
gnarled, straight—
tall tree standing,
I stare at light.

Genie Dailey
Jefferson, ME

Patterns
A sonnet

A single rose cannot the bush adorn;
One added would complete the symmetry
Of Nature's plan. A drifting leaf, forlorn
In flight, may peace enjoy and comfort see
When weather's whim companionship provides.
A shore is barren, stagnant, incomplete
Without a sail, a whis'pring of the tides.
A lonely man may also sense defeat
In having none with whom to share his plight.
But Solitude can outwit fickle Chance,
And his caprice put to ignoble flight.
The mind of Man will loneliness enhance
As singing Mem'ry carillons a blend
Of chimes in tune with feelings for a friend.

***

A. McKinne Stires
Westport Island, ME

Possessing

She handles life like a cocoon, gently,
   knowing the promise it holds.
She cradles love like a cocoon, hoping
   an unfettered thing will emerge.
As if her watching and holding
   could unravel the tangled bonds.
As if the thing were hers to own.

Leonore Hildebrandt
Harrington, ME

Spindrift and the Heart

No quick flashes, the minnows'
field of darts, only the clarified
form—a large fish, its cool shield
unhurried and slick as shadow,

sinking below the surface, away
from the waves' stacked wheels
tripping over themselves as they
topple and foam to the shore—

down to where plankton settles
like snow, where the pale creatures
scull and sift into a wide-mouthed
murky darkness—and here, below

the blood's agitation, to resume
again, to suppose translucence.

***

Sylvia Little-Sweat
Wingate, NC

Murrells Inlet

A lone pelican
sits on a weathered piling
drying feathered brine.

Robert B. Moreland
Pleasant Prairie, WI

Witch of November

The storm blows up quickly off the great lake,
waves peaking four and five feet crash the shore.
Daylight fades on this late fall afternoon,
darkness bringing with it the full-blown gale.
Hear the roar of a thousand waves as one
striking the granite, it permeates the
walls, rattling the panes, stirs fear in the soul.
Parka clad and gloved, the man struggles down
the gravel road to see the snow flurries
dancing in time in a lone mercury light.
The tempest is rising, snow blown with spray,
he stands alone above the breakwater.
To the north, Kenosha Harbor fades in
and out of view. Farther Racine obscured,
Wind Point Light warning of the reef beyond.
Temperatures plummeting, gusting wind chills
now near zero as waves toss ice daggers
borne on a demonic northeast wind. Three
weeks ago, Indian Summer's kiss held
promise for all who have known puppy love.
Forty-two years ago, the *Fitzgerald*
faced the crone, technology vaunted and
broken submerged, crew gone without a trace;
storm twice this bad. The witch is stealing tonight
whether prideful boater caught unaware
or lovelorn, starry eyed mate who waited
a bit too long to turn back towards home.

Phillip L. Radoff
Wayland, MA

Beach Buggy

It was one of those glorious summer days on the Cape, perfect beach weather. As he looked out at the cloudless sky, he heard the excited squeals of his three grandchildren anticipating a trip to the beach.

"And where might you be going?" he asked four year-old Jenny as she burst into the room in her new bathing suit, sandals, and floppy hat, struggling to prevent a pair of too-large sunglasses from slipping down her nose while clutching a plastic bucket and shovel in one hand and her favorite Raggedy Ann doll in the other.

"Me and Max and Ben are going to the beach. Mommy's taking us."

"Max and Ben and I," he corrected.

"Yeah, Max and Ben and I," she replied complacently. "You can come too, Grandpa."

"Thank you for the invitation," he replied. "It's a tempting offer, but I have things to do here today. Another time."

"What does tempting mean?" she asked, but before he could answer, his oldest grandchild entered the room and spoke up. He was fashionably dressed in Batman bathing trunks and Big Papi T-shirt, with contrasting Patriots cap. "What things do you have to do?" asked Max.

"Oh, you know, important grandfatherly things," replied his grandfather vaguely. Max looked at him skeptically, increasingly aware at the age of 12 that the remarks of elders could not always be taken at face value.

"I'm going, too," said the new arrival, nine year-old Ben, a cross between his older brother and a disheveled Peanuts cartoon character. Somehow, Ben's clothes never seemed to fit quite right. Shirts thought to be securely buttoned often came unbuttoned of their own accord, and shoelaces regularly untied themselves.

Phillip L. Radoff
Wayland, MA

"Well then," said their grandfather, "I hope you all have a splendid time. Are you going to drive to the beach?"

"No," they responded in chorus. "We're going to walk," said Max. "Mom's taking all the stuff we need in Jenny's old baby buggy."

"It's not my buggy anymore," exclaimed Jenny indignantly. "I'm not a baby. Why do we still have that old buggy anyway? There aren't any babies around."

"Of course not," her grandfather soothed, "but, you know, baby buggies can be very useful for carrying blankets and umbrellas and… and other things." He paused for a moment as a distant memory crossed his mind.

"Well, I do hope you have a good time," he continued, "but I also hope you remember the most important thing *not* to do when you get to the beach. Do you know what it is?"

The boys exchanged blank looks, but Jenny spoke up: "Don't go into the water until Mommy says so."

"Oh, that," scoffed Max, the worldly-wise. "That's for little kids. Anyway they have plenty of lifeguards."

"You know," mused their grandfather, "you can't always depend on lifeguards. Still, I'm really glad we have them at the beach. I can still remember the time when I was rescued by lifeguards. Did I ever tell you about that?"

"No!" they responded in chorus, attentive to the prospect of an interesting revelation from an unexpected quarter.

"Well I know you're in a hurry to leave, so maybe we'll save the story for another time. How would that be?"

"No, now!" they shouted again.

"Well, okay," he replied, "if you're sure you're not in too much of a hurry."

Assured of their attention, he continued, "I guess I must have been about Ben's age or maybe a little older. My mother and my brother and I were staying at a cottage in Atlantic City. That's in New Jersey, you know."

"Yeah, yeah, we know," said Max, who knew everything important there was to know.

Phillip L. Radoff
Wayland, MA

"My father was working except on the weekends when he came to visit, but he had to leave on Sunday night so he could get up in time to go to work on Monday morning. What I'm going to tell you happened on a weekday when my father wasn't there."

The children's grandfather paused a moment to collect his thoughts before continuing. "We used to walk to the beach every day, the three of us, my mother, my little brother, who was about Jenny's age, and I, taking turns pushing the baby buggy with all our stuff. Every day my mother would pick a spot near one of the lifeguard stands, spread the blanket, plant the umbrella, and hunt through her bag for the suntan lotion, but before she did all those things, she always said, 'Don't go into the water until I finish here and can watch you.'"

Three heads nodded in unison as he resumed his narration. "Well, you know what happens when you hear the same thing every day: after a while you don't pay much attention; it just becomes part of the background noise. You get to the beach, take off your sandals, look around to see if any other kids are nearby, and in the background someone says, 'Don't go in the water.' Sure, sure," he added, and glanced at Max, who smirked knowingly.

"On this particular day, the waves were pretty high because there had been a storm the day before, and we had to stay home. In other words, it was a great day for body surfing. When I looked around, there was just one kid nearby that I knew. He was a couple of years older than I was. I walked over to him, and he said, 'Hey, let's go out and body surf.' Well, what was I supposed to tell him? 'Sorry, I can't go. I have to wait for my mommy.' Not a chance. So we ran to the water and jumped in. It was pretty cold, but we got used to it and started swimming."

As he was speaking, he noticed his daughter in the doorway, also dressed for the beach and carrying a blanket and several towels. She opened her mouth to speak but thought

Phillip L. Radoff
Wayland, MA

better of it, curious to learn what was keeping her three children uncharacteristically absorbed, silent, and motionless, hardly an every day occurrence. Unnoticed by the children, she moved quickly to a corner of the room, deposited her bundles, and sat quietly, not wishing to break the mood. Her father glanced briefly at her and continued his narrative.

"I noticed right away that there was a strong undertow." Seeing the puzzled look on his granddaughter's face, he added, "An undertow, Jenny, is a current of water that pulls you away from the shore. Anyway, I swam out a short distance—at least it seemed like just a short distance—but the water was suddenly up to my shoulders, and I thought, 'That's far enough.' Earlier that summer my father had decided that I needed to learn the Australian Crawl stroke, and I had learned it well enough—or so I thought. I don't suppose you kids know what that is?" he said innocently.

"Sure we do," responded Ben. "We learned it in swimming class. You do it like this," and he proceeded to demonstrate with an impressive arm-over-arm movement. "And you kick your feet at the same time."

"Very good," replied his grandfather. "Well, you never knew my father, but he was an excellent swimmer and used to swim for miles every day when he was younger. So, naturally I began to do the Crawl and head for shore. At least, that was my intention, but I wasn't getting very far because of the undertow. I looked around for the other kid and saw that he was a lot closer to the shore than I was and swimming as hard as he could. Since my Crawl wasn't working, I tried some other strokes, but they weren't any better, and I wasn't getting any closer to the shore."

He glanced up and saw that there were now four pairs of eyes staring back at him, his daughter just as absorbed in the adventure as her children.

"I wasn't frightened," he continued, "not really—but I began to realize that it was going to be pretty hard to get back to shore on my own. Then I remembered the lifeguards and

Phillip L. Radoff
Wayland, MA

spotted them sitting on their high chairs and peering out over the ocean. I didn't want to make a fuss, but I thought it might be a good idea to get their help, so I began to wave. Then I called out to them—not a panicky shout, but calmly: 'Hey, there. Can you guys help me? I'm having some trouble'—at least, that's the way I remember it," he added.

"I never found out whether the lifeguards heard me or just saw some kid floundering in the waves in need of help. Anyway, before I realized what had happened, there they were, two lifeguards in a rowboat moving quickly toward me. One of them was holding a life preserver and calling out to me. 'Here, kid, grab this,' he said as he tossed me the big doughnut. I felt proud of myself for catching it on the first try. He pulled me quickly to the boat and lifted me in. I remember feeling kind of embarrassed and saying, 'Thank you,' as the lifeguards expertly maneuvered the boat around and headed for shore.

"By the time we got back, a large crowd had gathered to see what was going on. After all, you don't get to see lifeguards rescuing people every day, and I'm sure it was all very exciting. When I climbed out of the boat, everyone cheered—except my mother, who was screaming and crying and waving her arms, all at the same time. She didn't know whether to smack me for disobeying her or hug me for being safe. I think she did both. My brother just stood silently at her side, taking it all in and filing away the experience for possible future use, because you never knew what might happen to you."

Ben spoke up: "What happened to that other kid? Did the lifeguards get him, too?"

"I don't think they had to. I saw him in the crowd, watching what was going on, but he didn't say anything. He probably thought he'd get into trouble if he told his mother he had been out with me.

"I was fine. I kept telling everyone that I was fine—my mother, the spectators, and the lifeguards. I wanted them all

Phillip L. Radoff
Wayland, MA

just to go away and leave me alone. After all, when you stop to think about it, I had only gone for a little swim, had a little trouble, waved to the lifeguards for help, and they rowed out and pulled me in. All in a day's work. What was the big deal? But for some reason, the lifeguards and my mother didn't see it that way.

" 'Is he all right, is he really all right?' my mother kept asking. 'He looks all right, but I think you ought to get him home and make him rest for a while,' said one of the lifeguards. 'Do you have some way to take him so he doesn't have to walk?' At that, my brother spoke up—and I've never forgiven him for it. 'The baby buggy,' he said. 'We have a baby buggy.'

"The lifeguard nodded. 'Good idea. If you can manage it, put him in the buggy, take him home, and get him to bed—and keep an eye on him for the next 24 hours.'

" 'I'm not getting into any baby buggy,' I growled, glaring at my big-mouthed little brother. 'I can walk just fine.' But my mother was not to be denied. 'Shut up and get in,' she said, and I could see that I wasn't going to win *that* argument, so I got in."

The children looked at him incredulously. "Did you really have to get into the buggy," asked Ben.

"Indeed I did," replied his grandfather. "With my brother alongside and the beach stuff piled in around me, my mother began the trip back to our rental house, pushing the buggy along the boardwalk and then along the sidewalk. The return trip seemed a lot longer than the trip to the beach. I had my hat pulled down over my face so that no one would recognize me, but every now and again I heard a passerby snickering at the sight of a ten-year-old kid in a buggy. The girls with their giggling were the worst. I hated those girls. I hated my brother—and my mother. I hated the lifeguards. I hated everyone. I began to wish I had drowned. At least I wouldn't have had the shame of riding in a baby buggy.

"At some point our little parade passed a store with a

Phillip L. Radoff
Wayland, MA

large display window, and I got a look at my reflection, scowling and miserable in the buggy. 'That's it,' I said. 'I'm getting out.'

" 'Oh, no, you're not,' said my mother, but by now I was angrier than she was, and simply climbed over the side of the buggy and started walking quickly away, while my mother and my brother and the buggy followed. I wanted to get as far away as I could from that buggy and the awful embarrassment it represented. And so we arrived home. I refused to speak to my mother, threatened to kill my brother if he told anyone about my ride back in the buggy, rejected the glass of warm milk that the lifeguard had advised for reasons best known to him, and sulked for the rest of the day.

"The next day we went back to the beach with all our stuff piled in the buggy. No one spoke about what had happened the previous day. The water was calmer by then, and I went swimming, but not until my mother had finished spreading out the beach stuff and had come to the water's edge to watch as my brother and I splashed in the waves."

The three children had listened in fascination to their grandfather's account, trying to visualize the scene and to imagine themselves in similar circumstances. *What would they have done?*

Their mother stepped forward and looked quizzically at her father. "I don't think you've ever told me that story," she said. "I think I'd remember it."

"Oh, sure I have," he replied. "When you were a youngster. You've just forgotten."

Then he turned to the children and asked, "What do you think about that story?"

"Did it really happen or did you just make it up?" asked Max, ever the skeptic.

"I assure you, it's true," said his grandfather. "You can ask my brother the next time you see him. He'll tell you."

"Did he ever tell anyone else that you were riding in a baby buggy?" asked Ben.

Phillip L. Radoff
Wayland, MA

"I don't think so. If he had, I'm sure I would have heard about it," replied his grandfather. "I think he really believed I would kill him if he told."

"I guess you should have waited before you went into the water," reflected Max.

"Yeah," said Ben, "but that other kid was going in."

"You could have made up an excuse and waited," said Max. "That's what I would have done—and I wouldn't have gone out so far if there was an undertow. Didn't they have flags to tell you it was dangerous?"

"I don't think there were warning flags back in the old days. It was a long time ago. The lifeguards all wore long bathing suits and had handlebar mustaches and rode on unicycles," replied their grandfather.

"Now I know you're making *that* up," said Max.

"Yes, it wasn't that long ago. But the rest of it is true," he said and nodded solemnly. "Now I have a question for you three. You've heard what happened to me, so tell me what you are going to do when you get to the beach. Let me rephrase that: What are you three **not** going to do when you get to the beach?"

His daughter stepped closer, not wanting to miss a word of her children's responses. "Be careful when we go swimming so the lifeguards don't have to come and rescue us," said Ben, "and not go in before Mom says it's okay."

"Make sure Mom is watching before we go in the water," said Max, "and don't swim where the lifeguards can't see us," he added, practical as always.

"Those are all very good ideas," said their grandfather approvingly, glancing again at his daughter. She smiled and nodded at him. True or not, it was a great story to tell the kids.

Her father continued, "Because I'm sure you can see what might happen if you aren't careful."

"The lifeguards might not see you," said Ben, "or maybe they wouldn't get to you in time."

Phillip L. Radoff
Wayland, MA

"You could drown," said Max, and Ben nodded in agreement. Both boys fell silent as they contemplated the possibilities.

Just then, Jenny, who had been listening attentively to the exchange between her grandfather and her brothers, nodded vigorously, catching her grandfather's eye. Turning to her, he asked gently, "Jenny, you haven't said very much. What do you think about all this?"

With great solemnity the little girl replied, "I think we have to wait for Mommy, because…because if we don't… then we might have to go home in a baby buggy!"

"Yes, indeed," replied her grandfather. "That's exactly right, and that, Jenny, is why we still keep that old buggy, even though there aren't any babies around any more."

***

Irene Zimmerman
Greenfield, WI

Fledglings in Flower

Darkness dawdles
over the nest
where mother robin sleeps.

At her fledglings' peeps,
out she flies
to forage for insects.

Who taught them to wait
with beaks open wide—
a bouquet of lilies?

Jacinda Timmerman
Seagoville, TX

Waves of Grief

The wave rises behind me,
Crashing down with news that she's gone,
Simple words with tremendous force.

Hurricane waters swirl and pull me down.
Helpless, alone, in disbelief;
Thrashing, searching for some kind of relief.

Dazed and confused,
The weight of grief grabs hold and pulls me down.
An aching heart; it's hard to breathe.

An unseen Hand lifts my head above the water.
Full of sorrow I can't help but weep.
A lifeline held by loved ones appears before my eyes.
I find strength in the unseen and hold on for dear life.

Grateful to have the beach below me,
I struggle to my feet and continue my journey.
The mud sucks at my feet and pulls me down.
I trudge along, clinging to an unseen hand.

The ground seems firm;
A sense of normalcy returns.
Air again fills my lungs.

Another wave suddenly rises above me;
It crashes down, but is unable to sweep me away.
I find myself anchored by faith.
Resolute, I set my eyes before me.

Jacinda Timmerman
Seagoville, TX

The wave heads for shore once more,
But the tide doesn't reach as far as before.
A memory triggers a tear,
Special occasions without her near.

Another wave, I cry out "Abba!"
He wraps around me loving arms,
Whispering comfort and assurance.
I lean upon His strength and carry on.

A friend is swept to the deep by a wave.
I hesitate, still fearful of the water.
"God comforts us so that we can comfort others,"
Rang Paul to the Corinthians.
It was my turn to lend a hand and a shoulder.

I grit my teeth and head for the water,
Extending arms of love and support,
Tears mix in empathy,
Where once there would have only been sympathy.

Life is so uncertain,
Surprises and turns with no warning.
Still God is faithful and strong,
A towering Friend on which to lean,
A mighty Refuge in times of trouble,
The Giver of all good things.

A wave rolls in, gentler than before.
The water splashes my face,
Rolling down my cheeks.
I wipe the moisture with my palm,
Thankful the hurricane has calmed.

Jacinda Timmerman
Seagoville, TX

I look forward to the day
When the water brings more joy than pain,
A reminiscent smile
When cherished memories come to mind.
Dear to my heart she'll always be.

So I continue my journey,
Hand in hand with my Creator,
Until I cause my own wave
As I'm lifted to the sky
Where my Savior will wipe every tear from my eye.

***

Christopher Fahy
Thomaston, ME

Owls Head Harbor

Walking up the hill
from Owls Head Harbor
on a beautiful late June afternoon
the old white green-trimmed farmhouse
on my right with the rusty water pump
out front, all perfectly still
till I hear from within
the click of a cup against a saucer
and everything stops—including me—
and falls into place: the sun, the grass,
the flowers, the bay, the post office flag,
for just a few seconds,
and then moves on.

Augusta
Lakeside, Nova Scotia, Canada

It Takes a Village...

"It takes a village to raise a child." This ancient African proverb teaches an eternal truth. It does take a village, family, friends, neighbors, and children to nurture each of us. Islands, we are not.

These words "It takes a village..." have been coming to me this past week. My cousin and her partner left yesterday and this morning I took my youngest daughter to the airport. They each went the extra, caring mile.

Wintering in Tucson, I have lived in this mobile home for ten years. Each year I plan for unexpected repairs. I discovered a good "Mr. Fix It" by the name of Lance. Being independent by nature and having divorced "free help," I resolved never to ask for the latter. Then, if I can't do it myself after trying five times, I "call Lance."

This year, arriving here at four in the morning, I noticed when opening my door, that it caught on the deck. I pictured myself arriving next year not able to get in. With no car, no food and neighbors in dreamland, I would be sleeping under the stars. Then the next day, I also noticed little piles of dust in front of my deck steps. Thus, I comfort myself—after my visitors leave, I will "call Lance."

When my daughter arrives, she notices the deck needs painting—then notes the "spongy" bottom step. In two minutes she has the hammer, yanking it up. "No, you are not doing that on your vacation." A half hour later, at her insistence, the clerk at Home Depot looks at the step and states, "Ms., you have termites." This is the desert. *How is that possible?* We return home with the paint.

A day later my cousin and her partner arrive from Canada. He sees the missing bottom step. An hour later he is on his knees taking up two other steps—definitely termites.

Augusta
Lakeside, Nova Scotia, Canada

Then I ask him if I have a door problem. Now, he is under my mobile home, jacking it up to give it enough room to let the door swing freely.

Meanwhile, my cousin is on the computer showing me how to put my documents, writings, and pictures into the cloud. And my neighbor seeing the new steps, brings me over a geranium for decoration. Later, I was told another neighbor had brought over an electric saw to help get the job done.

My village also cared through the internet this past week. A friend "lends an ear" on Skype and several readers emailed their response to the latest writing, proving I am not posting into a vacuum. My six-year-old grandson comes alive on the iPhone and so do I as he excitedly exclaims, "Grandma, the snow is over your car and I am standing on the top step." Then he proceeds with a most enthusiastic and delightful description of a six-year-old's experience of snow. Quite unlike the adult descriptions I have heard recently.

What strikes me in it all is—I did not ask for help. In fact, there was no stopping my village even though, my answer was always, "No, I'll call Lance and do it later." Now I am sitting out here surveying my "estate" from my newly painted deck. Those termites are sprayed to death, my steps are solid; there'll be no sleeping under the stars next winter and my writings are saved in the cloud.

I feel gratitude's warm glow. I know what this week's writing is going to be—an eternal truth. Does it not take a village of people caring to nurture us, grow us and ignite our aliveness? This interaction reaches out far more than one might guess. Another light goes on in the universe and God winks again.

People caring—it does take a village.

Margaret Roncone
Vashon, WA

Miles at Sea

miles at sea
the lighthouse is a blink in the
eye of the great white
years ago I had you
tied to a floating dock
I wet my eyes daily
with salt water
not for you
but for thousands who would
never know your lazy walk
your hands holding two worlds
paths through woods
twisted our hearts
eventually we disentangled
frayed rope
sandy embankments
no foothold.

Karen E. Wagner
Ashland, MA

A New England Winter

I can smell the sharpness
in the air. A clear
hardness
still and crackling. The birds
are quiet. Dark wings
of a crow fly overhead,
silent for once.
Clouds are black, heavy
with flakes, white flakes
a lot of them jammed
like rumpled tissue
in a ball.
They hang low and
splintered by the
Northeastern wind.

Beginning to spit
shot gun pellets
of cold frozen rain.
Temperature's on a slide,
almost low enough
for snow and
falling fast.
Ground's covered with
slick sheet of ice
that defies snow tires.
Clouds closing in.
Sleet crusts
tree limbs.

Karen E. Wagner
Ashland, MA

First flakes falling
now,
sticking to fur
trimmed caps and
windshields
alike, disguising
the frozen sleet.
Wind's picking up.
Car headlights
covered by
snow, people walk
hunched against battering
gusts. Silhouettes
fade into the dark
of the encroaching
storm.

***

Paul G. Charbonneau
Rockport, ME

Night Life

When clouds fade away,
we see night as it is,
not so dark after all.
Stars wink at us
drop hints of a coming dawn
when darkness gives way
to first light
fully and finally
streaming through us all.

Peggy Trojan
Brule, WI

Blizzard

Half way through math class
all eyes are on
the tall south windows,
mesmerized by the huge flakes
picking up speed,
paying no attention to Mr. Berube.

By the end of the hour,
he stops the lesson,
announcing early dismissal.

We scramble to tidy our desks,
wash blackboards,
empty wastebaskets,
water the plant
on the science shelf.

Then we gather
to watch the storm
blowing out of Minnesota,
as though we had never seen
such frenzy and wait
for the buses,
everybody smiling.
A snow day tomorrow a sure bet.

Ilga Winicov Harrington
Waldoboro, ME

Searching Ichiban

Daisy peered down the mist shrouded train track in Yokohama. It was early morning and the train to Tokyo would be arriving any moment. The official part of their trip to Japan had ended the night before with a gala farewell dinner at the Yokohama Hotel where their Japanese hosts had ferried them from the week long *21st Century Genomics Conference* held at the Graduate University high on the hill above Hayama Shonen village.

Daisy turned to her husband Paul next to her on the platform. He had been one of the major figures invited to speak at the conference and she decided to tag along as a spouse. As always, she was neither fish nor fowl at these events. As a scientist in a related field, unlike other spouses, she attended most of the lectures. But as a woman, she was often suspect by the predominantly male contingent of the gathering. But now they were traveling on their own.

"Ready for another adventure, Paul?"

"Lead on madam tour director!"

"You remind me of Giles when he was young—that time he was chosen along with a little girl as volunteers at the aquarium show. When asked by the trainer to pet the killer whale, he promptly said into the microphone 'ladies first,' and incidentally brought down the house."

Daisy smiled at him even though she felt the familiar anxiety of coping in an unknown land with different customs. Neither Paul nor Daisy understood the language and most of the signs were incomprehensible.

A distant rumble announced the coming arrival of the commuter train. The crowd surged forward and they barely managed to squeeze on the train with their bags. All the seats seemed to be taken in the rail car. Daisy propped her suitcase against her leg in the crowded center and reached to

Ilga Winicov Harrington
Waldoboro, ME

hold onto the bar above her head only to feel a slight tug on her elbow. The black eyes of a wizened face peered out from underneath a mangled hat. The old woman's veined and bony hand reached out from an oversized earth-colored coat sleeve and tugged at Daisy's elbow again. She pulled her floppy bag on her lap and scooted over to make a place for Daisy on the crowded seat. Her high raspy voice seemed to give directions, but Daisy could only smile in acceptance and breathe a sigh of relief.

Her name really was not Daisy. The summer after her freshman year in college, on an outing with friends, she had picked daisies to make a garland and then fashioned it in a wreath for her hair. Her friends gave her the nickname "Daisy" and it stuck. She had always liked the uncomplicated and sunny feel of the name, preferring it to Ingelore. Now many years later, she still used it among friends and often on name tags at social gatherings. Except for publications and official documents, "Daisy" better suited her present life. So, "Ingelore" was conveniently tucked away, together with the brainy ugly duckling and past travels across many landscapes from war torn Europe. After all, what was one more *alias* for a person that had traveled so far?

Here she was once again, traveling in a strange country and still trying to make sense of her life. Daisy had always found that people, landscapes, events and even achievements in life were like thumbprint pictures from a trip. Those thumbprints kept collecting without the time to understand the whole. Someday she would assemble all those thumbprints to view the whole story, but for now—travel was enough.

She found people—watching on a Japanese morning commuter train especially fascinating. Besides the woman who had made room for her to sit, there was another tiny old woman next to her on the other side. A portly gentleman sat in the corner absorbed in his morning paper, but the rest of the coach was mostly young adults apparently on their way

Ilga Winicov Harrington
Waldoboro, ME

to work or school, predictably absorbed in their cell phones. Directly across was a most interesting exception. A teenage girl with a round face and long black hair, which gently swayed with the motion of the train, was totally absorbed applying her make-up. She raised a wand thick with mascara to her lashes, eyes wide open, repeatedly dipping her brush in the black liquid despite the movement of the train.

Daisy stared in fascination for a long while until a slight nudge made her turn. The old woman's eyes narrowed and her crumpled hat seemed to point towards the young girl along with her look of disapproval. In a little while the old woman lifted her chin, shook her head with indignation and gave Daisy's side another nudge. Her words came out low in a steady stream. Daisy had the distinct impression that her neighbor was "decrying the state of the younger generation," and expected her—even a foreigner—to agree. Daisy just smiled but the old woman persisted. Daisy, imagining her stern European grandmother could almost hear the words, *Such behavior on a public train! And she is young enough to still be in school. Where will it all lead?* The woman kept up her periodic comments and Daisy would nod and produce the occasional polite half-smile.

Half an hour later the train stopped. There was a rush to the exit and the girl across the aisle rose nonchalantly, her lashes like small black butterflies overshadowing her eyes. Daisy's opinionated neighbor parted with a warm smile and a small bow as to a friend.

They too disembarked and Daisy turned to Paul: "Well, that was most interesting."

"What was interesting?"

"I think," she mused. "I think I just had a conversation in Japanese."

"But you don't speak Japanese."

"No. But it's amazing how attentiveness can create understanding."

"Speaking of attention, how do we find the Shinkansen

Ilga Winicov Harrington
Waldoboro, ME

train to Kyoto?" and Daisy was brought back to their present situation.

They had procured all their train tickets at an English speaking travel agency at the Tokyo airport on first landing, but now they were overwhelmed with the seven-level Tokyo train station with multiple tracks. Their train would leave in half an hour, but signs or posted train schedules were no help. Daisy approached several other passengers standing on the platform; first one then another and another did not speak any English at all. Paul looked worried and Daisy was beginning to panic.

At that point a well-dressed woman in a maroon coat approached and asked, "Need help?" in fractured English. Daisy showed her the schedule and the tickets; unable to explain directions, the woman finally shook her head in exasperation and said: "You follow."

Three sets of stairs and innumerable platforms later they came to a gleaming silver bullet train—the Shinkansen—and the woman in the maroon coat showed their tickets to the train attendant who pointed to the correct steps ascending into the coach. Both Paul and Daisy bowed awkwardly to their "guiding angel" and offered profuse thanks, hoping to be understood. The woman smiled in response and leaving bowed gracefully.

They barely had time to find their reserved seats before the train slowly started to move out of the station. They were surprised that several of the passengers on the other side of the isle pulled down the shades on the window.

"Do you suppose they commute to Kyoto so often they don't want to see the scenery?" asked Paul.

"I can't imagine, maybe they stayed up too late last night and need a nap?" Daisy chuckled. "I'm going to watch for Mt. Fuji. We're supposed to pass it on this route."

"Good idea," said Paul settling more comfortably in his seat.

Once out of the station and beyond city limits, the train

Ilga Winicov Harrington
Waldoboro, ME

picked up speed, although you could not tell it from the sound or motion of the car. At 200 miles per hour the ride was very smooth, but it became extremely tiring watching the scenery flashing by out the window. They suddenly understood the wisdom of the drawn shades. It also was almost impossible to take any photos from the train, though Daisy managed to catch the top of Mt. Fuji sticking out above a layer of clouds, only because she was trying to snap an oncoming scene. By the time Paul got out his camera, they had gone miles down the tracks and the mountain had disappeared into the distance.

Kyoto was a bewildering city; fortunately the Hotel Nikko Princess was close to the subway lines, and large enough to have a staff with some ability to converse in English. Paul and Daisy started with a small city tour to give them some bearings and then set out on their own. They wandered throughout the city soaking up more than twelve centuries of history. There were imposing curved gates, temples and palaces. Daisy especially loved the gardens with moss covered paths enhanced by blooming cherries and camellias with curved wooden bridges over tiny streams leading to reflecting pools. They caught the monthly market at Toji temple with its mounds of yard long daikon radishes, countless bins of different dried fish and a gardener's paradise of small bonsai for sale.

Food was another adventure. Menus in English were available at the more expensive restaurants, but trying to eat like a Japanese businessman one day for lunch was humbling. After a morning tour of the Imperial Palace, Daisy spotted a noodle shop near the subway entrance and suggested a quick lunch.

The small shop was packed with young men on their lunch hour. The proprietor steered them to a small table in the center of the space and provided two Japanese menus, which fortunately had pictures of their special offerings. They managed to order using a form of sign language, or at

Ilga Winicov Harrington
Waldoboro, ME

least its gestural equivalent. Paul picked out a dish with udon noodles, egg and vegetables and Daisy chose one with soba noodles, with what appeared to be shrimp and vegetable tempura pieces on top.

In short order, two rather large bowls appeared at their table along with spoons and chopsticks. The liquid was steaming hot and the noodles refused to yield to the chopsticks without slurping. Their quick lunch rapidly became both embarrassing and messy.

Paul looked up across the restaurant and said sotto voice: "Don't look now, but we seem to be entertaining the clientele."

"How can I? Catching these noodles with chopsticks is impossible; they have a mind of their own!"

"Tell me about it. The udon noodles are worse!"

Daisy brushed back her hair and peeked. They seemed to be the focal point of all eyes in the restaurant; many of the young men had napkins politely dabbing their lips to keep them from visibly laughing. Had Daisy and Paul paid closer attention to those dining around them they would have seen that the trick to eating the noodles was to hold the bowl up to one's mouth and shovel the noodles across the rim before sipping the liquid.

When they finally finished, Daisy grinned and said to Paul: "Undoubtedly these guys will be able to amuse their coworkers all afternoon about our poor American table manners at the noodle shop." Humor was essential to survive travel.

On the third day it was Daisy's turn for professional contacts. When Paul accepted his invitation to Japan, Daisy immediately yearned to see Kyoto and all the ancient gardens. To justify the extended trip, she proceeded to obtain a seminar invitation from a scientist at Kyoto University, in her own research area.

When the invitation from Professor Ito arrived, Daisy had danced with glee.

Goose River Anthology, 2017//42

Ilga Winicov Harrington
Waldoboro, ME

Paul's eyes had only twinkled behind his thick horn rimmed glasses: "Why am I not surprised? Might have figured, how you would inveigle to see all those Kyoto gardens."

The day at Kyoto University arrived with the predictable difficulties in finding the right building and the professor's laboratories. The scientific community was reasonably versed in English and Daisy enjoyed answering the many questions from students and research fellows about her work after the seminar. Paul made himself comfortable in a chair and for a change played the role of accompanying spouse. Times like this required a tricky balance. Daisy knew from past experiences that given scientific discussions, where a couple were both scientists, people tended to preferentially seek the male opinion. Maintaining her own specialty was Daisy's way to minimize this problem and the day went well.

The evening with Professor Ito ended delightfully at a very old and traditional restaurant with scattered peak-roofed buildings around tiny courtyards, one featured a blossoming plum tree, the next a tiny pool reflecting a giant moss covered mushroom lantern, and another had a large sunken fire pit. The house specialty was tofu; everything from appetizers to desert was made with some type of tofu.

The following day they took an English guided tour to Nara. The day was clear and the Golden Temple was reflected with its picturesque pines in the large pond. Daisy and Paul marveled at the over fifty feet tall bronze statue of Buddha comfortably seated in the open pavilion. They strolled along the long moss covered walk with thousands of stone lanterns, which like the Buddha had sat there since the middle of the eighth century. One could not help but be awed by the stillness of the place and the passage of time.

"This looks even more impressive than the great Buddha Daibutsu we saw in Kamakura," said Daisy.

Paul only grinned: "I actually found that mountain of sake barrels against the hillside a lot more impressive."

During conference they had been taken on a trip to

Ilga Winicov Harrington
Waldoboro, ME

Kamakura, seat of the powerful twelfth century Shogunate that had split from the Imperial court in Kyoto.

"Remember also that immense camphorwood image of Kannon?" said Daisy. "The one with all those heads?"

"Eleven by my count—how bizarre."

"It's amazing that monk carved two of those images in the 8th century. The story goes he threw one in the sea to wash up in Kamakura, where supposedly it would save souls in need."

"How was it supposed to save souls?"

"They say each head would aid and guide humans to achieving different states of enlightenment." Daisy only wished that enlightenment was less difficult to discern among all the myriad thumbprints of modern life.

The Kamakura trip had been long on a misty and foggy day and full of surprises. During a free hour after lunch, they had taken a walk uphill to the saddest temple in Japan. The terraces leading to the Hasedera temple were lined with hundreds of small Jizō statues, for the salvation of souls of unborn children. Some of the pathetic statues were adorned with an offering of food or small toy in front of them—a poignant gesture. The experience made Daisy remember grief of close friends who had recently lost a child through miscarriage. She closed her eyes and pictured her two grown sons and she could only breathe *Thanks* for such a blessing.

In Nara their walk brought them to a deer park, where a herd of tame deer wandered among the visitors. Despite signs in both Japanese and English to be aware that tame animals with soulful eyes could bite, Daisy extended her hand with a saved breakfast roll toward one such creature. Paul readied his camera. Three deer immediately surrounded Daisy, each claiming a piece. Japanese deer were definitely not averse to western food.

"OW!" Daisy suddenly whipped around.

Paul bent over laughing and the camera shots went wild.

"Shoo, you impolite creature." Daisy waved her arms

Ilga Winicov Harrington
Waldoboro, ME

frantically.

Another soulful eyed creature, unable to partake of her food offering had partaken of Daisy's *derriere* from behind. It was time to go.

They spent their last morning at Ryōan-ji. It was still early morning and the crowds had not yet arrived at Kyoto's ultimate dry Zen garden from the late 15th century. The path led up to a low building with a long veranda and an overhanging roof. In front of the building stretched a raked sea of white sand in which fifteen placed stones seemed to float serenely, according to some master design. Beautiful, yet the garden was designed so one could never view all the stones together, thus seeing the perfection of the design in it's entirety. Daisy fleetingly recognized the need to capture these moments, took a deep breath and sat down.

They sat on boards at the edge of the veranda and gazed silently out on the peaceful scene. The neighboring trees cast shadows that moved languidly across the sand, a bird called in the distance. Daisy and Paul had the place to themselves, until the sound of approaching voices broke the silence, convincing them to end their time in this perfect place.

At the Tokyo airport, waiting for their flight back home, Daisy toyed with a small cat figure wearing a kimono that she picked up in a crafts shop. She thought about her recent thumbprint experiences and her disappointing search for a real geisha. They had gone to Gion, Kyoto's Geisha District, to search for a traditional tempura restaurant one evening. It was dusk, they were just ready to cross the bridge, when she appeared at the other end. Her mincing steps were likely taking her to a party, since she carried a beautifully wrapped gift under her arm, with a big bow matching the colors of her obi. She was perfect from her apricot kimono with the multicolored obi, black hair gleaming high held in place with bamboo and white stockings peeking from the traditional shoes. On closer view, the nostalgic picture shattered—she

Ilga Winicov Harrington
Waldoboro, ME

was talking on a cell phone as she walked!
    Daisy had to acknowledge that some thumbprints were disappointing. And yet, like the Zen garden had taught her—even partial views were beautiful, if imperfect.

***

Sharon Lask Munson
Eugene, OR

First Light

I wake to the high-pitched sound
of an early morning freight train—
too late to fall asleep again,
too early to rise.

I follow the sun
as the changing light
refashions my walls,
transforming pale ivory
into an incandescent mauve.

From open windows
I inhale an earthy smell
from last night's rain.

The neighborhood screech owl
will soon stop hunting
and silently fly home to roost

as the western meadowlark
tenders me a cheerful good morning
with its flute-like song.

Ellen M. Taylor
Appleton, ME

Velveeta, 1977

Top shelf, beside the leftover casserole,
bigger than a box of Girl Scout cookies:
Velveeta cheese. We sliced it like Spam
for lunch, sliced it thin on Ritz crackers for
company, or cut it into chunks to hide a pill
for Bucky, our shaggy Golden Retriever,
rescued from someone's dank basement.
At the White House, Jimmy Carter
put up solar panels. Love Canal
was declared a Federal Emergency.
At our house, we had a chimney fire
from burning green wood. My father
lost his job, but we never felt any
emergency. On meatless Fridays
he made Rum Tum Tiddy, a Depression
favorite at his childhood house.
My five brothers and sulky teenage sister
would gather in the kitchen while he
warmed tomato soup, poured it
over toast, crowned with Velveeta
and a dash of Worcestershire sauce.
"A nutritious meal!" he'd pledge
with his wooden spoon and a flourish
like the red banner on the Velveeta box:
designed to keep everyone growing, healthy,
and strong. And my father, aproned
and humming, was never wrong.

Deb Stout
Waldoboro, ME

The Angel Dance

Once upon a moonlight walk
    I saw an angel pass.
I called to her; she looked my way
    As she danced upon the grass.
Her eyes were violet stars of light,
    Her gown a golden hue,
Her crown of curls swung from her face
    As she twirled upon the dew.
I could not move my eyes away
    And tried hard not to blink
So fluid were her Angel wings
    Like a nectar—too precious to drink.
She smiled as bright as a sun could shine
    As she moved toward me through the night,
And with her grace I knew her love
    And felt her strong white light.
"Are you here for me?" I heard her say,
    And I said I didn't know.
I'm on a path that's winding fast
    And I'm not sure where it goes.
She said, "When faced with uncertainty,
    It's best to take it slow—
Stop and dance for a while, right where you are
    You've plenty of time to know.
Now is the only time you own;
    Your path won't go away—
And when your music moves you on,
    You'll know the tune it plays."
As I listened to her soothing words,
    My body seemed to float
And I moved slowly with the wind

                                      (continued)

Deb Stout
Waldoboro, ME

Like soft sails on a boat.
Turning and feeling the dew on my toes
    Lifting my arms up high
Swaying and dancing the time away
    Under the warm night's sky.
I knew the words she gave to me
    Were presents, gifts of truth
And if I danced in golden time,
    Moments I would never lose.

***

Richard Taylor
Bethel, ME

Echo Taps for Father

I steal from my bed to the top of the stairs
when the lights turn down in my bedroom
and his banjo tunes to the shade
beneath his smile.

I find my balcony seat in high half-view
of the stage below. Softly he sings
things a shadow only says to the fingers
of a calloused hand

to smooth the halting syncopations
of his haying days, lift his late diminuendo
into melody and soothe the night with the lilt
of his long company.

Now whenever my light turns off
I take my seat at the top of the stairs,
and I call back to him.

Goose River Anthology, 2017//49

the late Edward O. Barsalou
Kittery Point, ME

October

The leaves change and the sun has become miniscule.
The birds scramble for their feed.
The squirrels compete.
I am glad to be here, alone in my little place.
The world outside has become difficult for me to bear.
When I was young, I had a need to compete.
The cost did not matter, only how fast you shuffled your feet.
Now, my feet are tired.
My legs no longer wish to travel at those speeds.
My grandchildren thrill me most.
Like everything else, time will stop for no one.
Yet, I feel it has slowed for me.
I am glad to be here, alone in my little place.
I'll whittle out more words,
Hoping for my saving grace.

***

Robert B. Moreland
Pleasant Prairie, WI

Referendum

Sudden downpour like God's own tears
brings a flash flood. She huddles with him
stubborn rock of a man determined to go.
Ford truck clunks in reverse, windshield wipers
drone in time with flashes of lightning. They go to vote
having researched their lack of choices on the Internet;
his love of country borne of honor and duty,
her love for him transcending his stubbornness.

Mary Jane Mason
Larchmont, NY

Jack

On a grey March morning in 1902 Jack Edwards, his wife Emma and their six children stood alongside the open grave of Mary Reilly. Mary Reilly's six children stood opposite. Mary's husband Eoghan was dead five years. Mary Reilly and Jack Edwards had been sister and brother and had lived in the same Brooklyn neighborhood all their lives. As Jack and Emma walked slowly from the grave and out through the churchyard gate, he gathered in Mary's six children and took them home.

"Jack, we've hardly enough space for our six," whispered Emma.

"What else can we do, Mother?" he asked as they opened the front door.

"You're right of course," she sighed. "The boys will go in with John, the girls with Lily and the older girls in the attic room."

Even a stone cutter's salary hobbled Jack's ability to support twelve children. He worked overtime and put less in his lunch pail. "Mother," he said one day, "I need help with the money. I know several families over on Flatbush Avenue. They are good people and they'll take in our four oldest girls as domestics."

"Oh Jack," Emma gasped.

A long look from Jack told her he was right. "Of course they'll come home on weekends," he added, trying to soften the blow.

Too soon the day came. Jack hitched up the buggy and loaded the girls, each with her own valise, and the youngest, Lily into the ancient vehicle. "You can come along for the ride," he told Lily. Slowly they made their sad but determined way down the avenue, leaving the girls with their new employers. When they'd left the last one, Jack and Lily rode

Mary Jane Mason
Larchmont, NY

down to the park and stopped the buggy. They sat there. Lily began to cry. Jack began to cry. "What are we gonna do Lily?" he asked over her head as he hugged her.

Finally, he turned the buggy around and started back up the avenue, stopping along the way and reclaiming his girls.

As Jack walked in his front door with the girls he found the dinner table set with fourteen plates.

***

Manny Fiori
San Francisco, CA

Train Tracks

Sitting at the Amtrak train station
Nicole jumps up down and sways, all excited
She sees him coming, she's all get up and go!
She stops long enough to voraciously inhale
A Marlboro Light

Their eyes meet with a precipitous stare
His chest heaves, her heart flutters with
A little rock breeze in seven seconds
Not knowing which way to turn

Her words are all tongue tied
In mid air stumble
Nathan's hearts on idle, they stare

At each other across
The train tracks.

Laura Rickards
Bayville, NJ

The Great Northern Woods

It was a vacation that created a sensation of loss of space and time, an escape from the place that we call home, and retreat from the mundane conditions and constraints of our daily lives.

In the thin vale of early morning haze you could just make out the pine topped mountains. The pine grew to the water's edge—tall, proud, and green. Some colored so dark green that they look black, and others light enough that they were almost lime. Musical calls of birds filled the sky. The water was still and clean. Minnows darted about, and pebbles of many shapes, sizes and colors decorated the basin of the lake and added more for the eyes to behold. Minutes turned into hours, hours into days and a week of bliss. At any hour of the day, the woods brought delight. These Great Northern Woods were full of life.

Jascha, almost eleven-years-old had not changed his boxers for nearly four days, which indicated that even with a nightly reminder, his teeth had not likely been brushed for the same. A messy, enthusiastic eater, the menu for the week could be read upon his gray, cotton shirt—beef oil, mustard, ketchup, coffee, watermelon, barbecue sauce, a spot of now soured milk and a gooey, marshmallow glob holding pine needles and other earthly debris, wrapped in sweet deliciousness. There was also one wrinkled, dried, and quite stuck kernel of corn at the hem of his shirt.

When hate has multiplied and we are successful at killing ourselves over some insanity about oil, water, land, food or God, life will be born again in a place like this. Perhaps the spirit of this little boy will evoke a time of simplicity and innocence and a few survivors will make new within the sweet pine.

Jascha, come, sit, listen to the sounds distant and near. Can you hear? Can you hear the pine growing?

Thomas Peter Bennett
Silver Springs, MD

Traps

Fog at dawn reveals
    Spiders' web craft.

A dewy sheetweb
    Links grass blades
        And girds weed stalks.

Tension-web filaments
    Tether tree branches.

Filmy domes disperse
    Reflected light from
        Sticky capturing webs.

Attending each web,
    A spider eagerly awaits
        An insect snack.

First published in *Encore Seasons* by **Goose River Press**, 2017.

T. Blen Parker
Richmond, ME

Queen Kennebecca

Visitors once stood in awe
on her mossy banks
where the wild rice grows.
Viking explorers and Merchant Adventurers
seeking improved trade routes,
sailed next to prisoners eager to
renew lives in a wild country, beside
slaves traveling the underground railroad,
each riding quietly upriver
via Queen Kennebecca,
en route to Canada.

Queen Kennebecca, a lifetime supporter
of worldwide trade between Abenaki Chiefs
adorned in beads and feathers,
during fiery sunrises or sunsets
along her riverbanks in Maine,
or merchants arriving from a continent away.
Toasting with cocktails brimming with
ice-cubes gleaned from Queen Kennebecca's
pristine waters, European ladies
fondled iridescent beads fashioned
from shells by Abenaki maidens
across the ocean in New England.

Ladies on Swan Island in Maine, residing
along Queen Kennebecca's shores
drank French wine
from Italian crystal goblets
at tables set with Irish linen,
dined from English silverware,

(continued)

T. Blen Parker
Richmond, ME

enjoying exotic spice dishes from India
served on Chinese porcelain,
by young maidservants
from Chad or Bermuda.

Mesmerizing scores, the ageless Queen
spans hundreds of years
across thousands of piers.
Her commanding presence continues
to flow smoothly linking people,
cities, merchants, and products
emerging from the deepest forests
of Maine, touching continents
across the sea and back.

King Pines marked with a broad arrow,
harvested from the Queen's shores,
sold downriver as sturdy masts
on great sailing ships, or destined for
building mills, churches, and new homes.
Native baskets of sassafras,
hops, herbs, and wild berries
overflowing, shipped on to London.

Cod and sturgeon salted,
drying on flakes in the sun,
wheat milled, game hunted,
mink and beaver trapped,
traded in ports across the sea.
Queen Kennebecca offers abundance,
uniting people, continents, countries,
her compassion as fathomless as
the depth of a mother's love.

Christina Marsden Gillis
Berkeley, CA

Red Rock: A Real-Life Parable

(Whoever) causes this inscribed stone to be removed [or] throws it into the water...upon this man may the great gods...Look wrathfully.
—Inscription on ancient Babylonian boundary stone.

When he asked me to help him carry the heavy L.L. Bean canvas bag down to the shore, I didn't have to know what was in it. He'd lived just down the hill from us, between our property and the Carters' field, for years; helping out was just what one did.

Now here we were, two old guys carrying a bag containing a rock painted bright red. We didn't talk much. We were already part way along the path, just approaching the spot where the elder bushes block out the view of the bay, when he said, "I shouldn't have painted it red. Now I just want to get rid of it, dump it into the sea."

I couldn't answer much to that. I recognized the rock and remembered that the bright red paint had looked like blood rising up in the surrounding grasses. There's a lot of rock on a small island in Maine. I thought about all the rock that is not red, rocks in old tumbling walls, in empty foundation holes, in the giant slabs that mark the edges of the island itself. Not to mention the rock beneath the ground on which we were walking, the deep, and deeper, layers that literally support us.

But Ed—that's my neighbor—needed to talk about the rock he had painted red. He did it only to mark his property line, he said. But it had to have been more than that. There was the anger that had been boiling for several summers. It had distilled into pure venom. Disputes about property boundaries on a small isolated island produce this kind of anger. It gnaws at you. That's what the red rock was about.

He had placed it on his northern boundary where it was sure to be a red flag to Andy Charles. Charles was his neigh-

Christina Marsden Gillis
Berkeley, CA

bor (a relative of Ed's no less). He had particularly ugly temper–and a feeling about property that pretty much matched Ed's. I remember the day Andy Charles told me he didn't like my wife's body language as she glanced at his blueberry patch: "I can tell she plans to steal my berries," he had said. He was difficult, no doubt about it. His taunts and loud curses were all too well known on the island, especially to anyone who disputed his claim that the path in front of his house, a right-of-way for a hundred years, was now his to control. Yes, the right-of-way runs only a hundred feet or so in front of Charles' living room bay window, but most of us wouldn't object to one or two folks a day going by, especially when it's the same families who've been here for at least fifty years.

"For the eighty summers I've been coming to the island that path has been a right-of-way," Ed kept saying. "Besides, I have to use it to get to my spare wood lot."

We all knew that lot too. It's the one Ed had carefully marked off with tall wood stakes. That was before he painted the survey pipe, and more importantly, the adjacent rock–part of which may have been on Andy Charles' property—right red.

Not that there's anything unusual about rocks and boundaries. We have one at the southeast corner of our front field. It's a big round rock with a hole in the middle, hard to see in the thicket of juniper and wild blackberry bushes. But we'd never think of painting it. We know that our neighbors on that side feel attached to the island just as we do; exact boundary lines don't matter. It's the trust that's important, the sense that the land has a kind of sacred quality. It's bigger than we are. That's really the point. It's like those ancient Babylonians who believed that the gods oversaw the land, and boundary stones only marked the trust accorded different groups to maintain particular spaces. The rocks weren't about ownership. After all, the people in those tribes would at some point disappear; but the stone would-

Christina Marsden Gillis
Berkeley, CA

n't. And shouldn't.

The rock that Ed placed on his boundary must have belonged once to the dark foundation of the island. That's why it had glowed so unnaturally red in the field. It didn't belong there and maybe didn't want to be there either. I thought of it as having a hidden consciousness, holding secrets that we will never know. A poet who lived years ago on our island called rocks the first "historians," never "inexpressive, unyielding, [or] immobile." I like what she said, the idea that when the rocks have agency the land is a sacred trust. I guess that's what the Babylonians thought too. Prying up the stone and painting it bright red to mark out private property is breaking the trust.

In fact the 200 years of the known history of our small island have seen some pretty highly charged disagreements over property lines and access. There are lots of old stories: the man who sliced off the tail of another man's cow in retribution for some now unremembered slight to his land, the barn that mysteriously burned down. Then the day came when no one could make a living any more on the island, and it was left to stand by itself through all the winters, guarded only by its granite borders. The summer people took over, repaired the old crumbling houses or built new ones, tried to figure out their property lines based on ancient deeds, and as one would expect, got into disputes. Wounds were inflicted that would take years to heal. And some never did.

Ed knew about that history. He'd even been part of it. For years he'd carried on a vendetta with another neighbor over a blueberry patch on the north side of his property. I remember those days. "The great blueberry wars," some of the old islanders said. When, at an advanced age, the other property owner died and his heirs chose not to continue the battle, the blueberry patch, no longer a bone of contention, grew wild. The property stakes Ed had installed to mark his line bleached and rotted under a succession of winter blasts and summer suns.

Christina Marsden Gillis
Berkeley, CA

    Then came Andy Charles to occupy the property just east of Ed's land. No one had known anyone quite like him. His property was a kind of cocoon where he could bury himself and keep the world out. Within a couple of summers, boundary stakes and signs began to appear, then the surveillance cameras, five to be exact, lurking in the branches of his apple trees, attached to both front and back doors, and mounted in a stump on the far side of the right-of-way with a clear view of would-be trespassers or of anyone, like my wife, even looking at his precious blueberries.
    But we were already well on our way down the path to the shore by this time, and I didn't say any of these things to Ed.
    Instead: "Too bad you used the same red paint that everyone sees on your barn door."
    Ed didn't answer. He was lurching forward, struggling with his share of our load. I had to hustle to keep up with him. He was desperate to rid himself of the rock. It was freighted with bad memories, all the stupid actions that had brought only grief and frustration, all the property stakes and markers he had put in place. Stabs of pain were moving from his shoulder and down his arm. Yes, the pain came from the heavy load, but I knew it was deeper than that.
    By now we had reached the path that leads directly to the island's dock. But we didn't want to go that way. It was almost a full tide, the only time when the dock is usable, and we were likely to see other neighbors there, all heading off to do errands on the mainland. We might even see Andy Charles, the very last person we wanted to meet. No, on this day, carrying this burden, we didn't want to see anyone. Better to leave the main path and cross the field that borders the shore.
    It didn't matter that our feet left an ugly rough scar in the blanket of daisies and black-eyed susans that fill the field in mid-summer. We didn't even notice. We saw only the ocean, clearly in view just beyond the belt of granite that seemed to sparkle in the bright sun.

Christina Marsden Gillis
Berkeley, CA

This was the rocky margin that still had to be crossed. It would be difficult with our heavy load, and I was dreading it. But we couldn't afford to lose momentum now. We had to keep moving forward. The rock in the bag was swinging crazily between us. With each step, it seemed to get heavier with the anger, fear, and tension concentrated within it.

Looking back on that day, I think Ed and I must have looked like a pair of drunken lemmings, holding our unwieldy load, and struggling to cross the granite slab that marks the border between land and sea. We were neither of us young, and this was no time for a fall. We took a moment, though only a moment, to put the bag down and regain our balance. Then, haltingly, we stumbled forward once again, the sea drawing us on toward the granite's edge. The wash of the surf, pushed by the incoming tide, told us we are almost there.

In only seconds, though it seemed much longer, we reached what you could call the end of the island. Or maybe it was the beginning. It's hard to tell on an island, but a margin in any case. An almost-full tide boiled below us.

"Now I'll be rid of it," Ed muttered. In his voice I heard not triumph but relief.

There was nothing left to say. We gathered our strength, fumbled once again to balance ourselves on the rough surface of the granite, and hoisted the rock out from the bag. Panting, straining, we lifted it up. And with one final effort we hurled it into the sea.

The rock hit the water with a raucous splash and rapidly sank to the bottom. Small ripples circled outward from the spot. We peered down into the ocean's murky depth. One rock stood out from the others tumbled there. It still glowed blood red.

Diane Colvin Reitz
Panacea, FL

Lost in Thought

Looking over its
warm, caramel color,
my coffee cup speaks
to me about the
upcoming day.

The clouds of steam
float up and cascade
'round my head in circles
to help me breath.

Holding the cup
with both hands,
the coffee fragrance
makes love to my
memories, pulling
all my pieces together

warming another day
for one who has emptied
this cup and a thousand
cups, poured gently over
milk, white sugar cubes

and many lost thoughts.

Mark Biehl
Hales Corners, WI

Mirror

Who are you?
How dare you
Confront me
With this face
Of age?
Not mine.
No way.
You lie!

I am years younger
With a past of great adventure
And agile joy.

A past with unending vigor
And promises of dreams and longings.

I will not grow old.
I will never succumb to
Those rituals of assisted existence
And slow retreat.

After all,
AARP reflects graceful slowing,
A smiling, effort-free sunset!

I've paid my dues—
So why do you taunt me
With this failing image?

Robert R. Witte
Waldoboro, ME

Once Again

Like an aged bear
shaggy and bewildered
by the Spring sunlight,
I venture forth.
The stale air of my den
gusting out into
the freshness
I am almost afraid
to savor.
Still I live.

***

Laureen Haben, osf
Milwaukee, WI

Finding Gold

In the tiny hamlet of Piedmont, Italy
when the weather is "just so"
with dried leaves covering the ground

and led by a dog having a special sense of smell
who can find down only a few inches
as he digs in the soil

a single piece precious beyond words
loved for its fragrance but more for its taste:
the white truffle.

Rippling Out

The sound ripples out from my deepest self,
a wellspring of faith and delight.

What does the sound say?
"Go forth," it says.

"Go forth and still this ocean of disorder,
these waves of dismay."

"Live in the now," the sound says,
"the now of creation and hope."

I shudder as the words are spoken.
The ocean's so vast, the waves so great.

I fear. This distance is far.
Instead, I float, languid in relaxation.

The water holds me. I am contained.
Peace spews out. The waves still.

The sound is silent.
I am at peace.

Sandy Conlon
Steamboat Springs, CO

Stay Awhile

How long can you stay
There is so much to do
The sorting and casting away

Please don't leave just yet
For in this house of flesh and bone
There is still too much I can't forget

Rooms filled with children's play
The beauty of a summer day
Every place that love was near

We built a bond steady and strong
Sheltering our home
From the fiercest storms

Rooms filled with words
When we finally understood
Grew heavy with silence

How long will you stay
As you lie quietly looking at us
Tethered now to the air we breathe
By plastic tubes giving and taking away

We wait and watch
Grateful for your life
Transformed forever in your dying.

Judith Andersen
Owls Head, ME

In the Garden

Our family backyard, circa 1950's in Oak Park, Illinois was a simple thing—little different from those of our neighbors. Forsythia, bridal wreath, and mock orange bushes clustered around our Victorian house. Hollyhocks lined one backyard fence, but did not give enough coverage to block out our rather bohemian neighbor who weeded in her garden each morning wearing a nightgown, but that is another story.

A source of great pride was the line of peonies, pink, white, deep rose, and candy cane, planted in front of the garage. Mom tried her hand at a variety of lilies in the garden along the right-hand fence, but was most successful in a small plot next to the garage where her beloved violets and lilies of the valley thrived. Unfortunate, we kids thought, was her success with rhubarb in that corner; Grandma loved to make conserves and tonics, pouncing on the purple stalks as they came up.

Although there might be an occasional dusting of fertilizer, mulch was generally not heard of. The midwest rarely sported many perennials, but leaned toward the baby's breath-geranium-pansy school of thought. These occasionally sat under the bushes which accented our generous Queen Anne's porch.

...and there was the grass, front and back, just waiting to be mowed with the hand-pushed mower and weeded with that funny forked metal stick. We children were conscripted as soon as we were tall enough to push and focussed enough to recognize a weed and act on it. Raking in Autumn could be fun as we made huge piles which we could use for jumping into or hiding. Bad boys sometimes came by with a match and set them on fire, but gardening was generally a quiet job. Our yard was a refuge in the hot summers.

My husband and I live in Mid-Coast Maine in an associ-

Judith Andersen
Owls Head, ME

ation on a small cove. Friends always exclaim that we must love the peace and quiet of our surroundings. We gulp and agree, but they are rarely here when all hell breaks out. As four to five heavy trucks from one contractor roar in to attack three properties, I find myself reciting a poem memorized in high school, "The Assyrian came down like a wolf on the fold..." Soon two unusually loud leaf blowers bellow from a new group of workers who arrive next door, causing me to run out of our kitchen on the opposite(!) end of the house to see what explosion has taken place. The fellows handle the blowers with the panache of fencers. Apparently, rakes are passe. Another starts up. ROAR, ROAR, ROAR FOR HOURS. Time for ear plugs or a drive away from home.

The new doctrine of landscaping apparently states that if a little mulch is good, truckloads must be better. BEEP, BEEP, CRASH, and one load is delivered, and there are many more to come—oh, and lots of fertilizer to follow. Things really pick up in Spring and Fall, though many are away in their other homes and cannot enjoy the melee. Starting at 8 am, they whine away for a six hour concert. *Shall we get rid of offending boughs and branches?* they think. Perfect job for a chainsaw! WHAA, WHAA, WHAA. Then the natural order of things is to use the chipper. CRACKLE, ZING, BANG, CRUNCH. Everyday in summer someone, someplace, is using a gasoline or electric mower. DRONE, DRONE, DRONE. When the machines quiet down, shouting and loud radio music blasts. The latter is not Mozart.

The 18th century English landscape architect, Capability Brown, "England's greatest gardener," created vast orderly landscapes of hills and valleys, ponds and streams. How did he do it? His workers used spades, axes, saws, rakes, scythes, shovels, wheelbarrows, horse drawn wagons and other simple equipment. Sheep were used to cut the grass and stamp down clay and soil—lucky neighbors, gorgeous results, much less noise, methinks.

Julia Rice
Milwaukee, WI

Hawk and Mouse

The proud hawk stares off into the air,
head up, wings wrapped around his body,
arrogance gaping.
Talons emerging from soft feathers,
lie silent against the whiteness.
Like Jesus in the Temple, he knows rightness
and is about to fly

while the mouse in the house
tries to sell us with his cuteness.
He stretches long, curls into a seductive ball.
On the move constantly along the baseboard,
he expands lithely and profits playfully,
eating and hiding and defecating.

So justice offends us with its strictures,
its arrogance. It shows its rightness.
It confronts our complacence
and whips and overturns those

who charm us into buying their doves,
lure us into purchasing nonsense that costs less
that piles up in our corners and fills our pantries,
deceiving us with stuff to fill their pockets,
ruining the food of the poor with their poop,
using us to make their lives rich.

In spring the hawk carries off the mouse
and the heavens reflect its justice.

Rena Winters/Ron Corbin
Las Vegas, NV

Tell My Wife I Love Her

No suspect had been seen, no warning expected
From ambushed shots that were fired.
But I saw my partner's slumped and lifeless body,
And feared our situation was dire.

The windshield had been shattered
By the cowardly act of an assassin's aim
Accelerating the police vehicle as trained.
I quickly sped-out of the killer's lethal frame.

Once relieved of no more looming peril
I pulled to the curb and screamed into the mike,
Officer Needs Help! Officer Down! Shots Fired!
Only then fear started to dissipate and my anger spike.

Blood oozed from a fatal throat wound,
My partner's blood saturated his uniform of blue.
The metallic shine of the badge losing its luster
The red, warm, liquid of life turned a purple hue.

Holding-up my partner's head and
Brushing from his cheeks glass shards,
He whispered, "Tell my wife I love her."
And with eyes wide open, his last breath expired.

My partner had survived military service
In mid-east and hostile foreign lands.
What irony for a war hero to die at home
By gutless and cruel, cold-blooded hands.

The memorial had a line of mourners stretched long
One of life's heartbreaks, a tragedy that was so wrong.

Rena Winters/Ron Corbin
Las Vegas, NV

* "Tell My Wife I Love Her" is based on a personal experience of a police officer who lost his partner in the line of duty. In these harried days of charges of police harassment and unlawful violence by ordinary citizens our country is torn apart. With hopes that in the future people of honor, law and order, which we must have to be a great country, will come together with love and peace.

***

Robert B. Moreland
Pleasant Prairie, WI

Through a Glass Darkly

Huge CAT scan whirs. "Take a breath," she prompts while
the faded picture of sunlit fall trees
seems surreal. What is it that lurks inside him
unseen, growing; robber of hopes and dreams?

Technician, pleasant, smiles uneasily,
dissecting by the slice; showing no hint
of what it might be. Not her job to be
the one who upends his reality.

So much taken for granted, now
face mortality, the grim reaper smiles.
Done, go and change for the next test,
indignity of hospital gown, exposed.

All of his life dedicated to cancer research
never did he dream it would come to him.
Will he ever understand why? Through darkest glass,
x-rays reaching beyond the tissues, he sees.

Karyn Lie-Nielsen
Waldoboro, ME

Rites of Passage

You're fourteen,
the new car hop at the Dairy Castle Drive-In.
It is nineteen sixty-eight and the heat is on.
Your brother has been drafted into the army.
Leaving in a few days to fly Hueys
over jungles a million miles away.
He won't be coming back.
Meanwhile, trying to secure collapsible trays
onto car doors modeled after the Edsel,
you spill each one. Contraptions
clatter to the gravel like gunshots.
Root beer, French fries, cheeseburgers, wasted.
Ketchup, smelling metallic and salty,
drips on the driver's side
of each vehicle you serve.
Children in the back seat
don't know whether to laugh or cry.
From your point of view, the ground
looks like something on the six o'clock news.
Squares of paper napkins lift from the crash site
like thin handkerchiefs you might have used
if you had only known
what was going to happen.

Jennifer Clements
Vinalhaven, ME

Chicken Dumplings

"Mom could have killed someone."

Stopped at a red light, Georgia looks across at her sister as if to say, come on, Maggie—there's no way.

"If she can't back up in a parking lot without crashing into somebody, then she could just as well pull out in front of a school bus on the freeway and, bam, fifty dead kids. If I hadn't flown out, you'd have ignored this, wouldn't you?"

Georgia asks if they can please not fight.

Heaven forbid they should fight. Maggie has learned in AA to stop expecting people to think like she does. She's confrontational; she knows that. And her resolutions for calm fall apart when she's with her sister. They drive past grand old homes with autumn foliage. No relation to the trailer perched on New Mexico's red earth where Maggie drank her morning coffee. She hopes Harris will fix the leak in the kitchen ceiling while she's gone. Not that she would trade there for here, even though this exclusive neighborhood is as confusingly familiar as the sound of her mother's voice.

They pull up behind their mother's battered blue Honda and get out. Maggie is surprised by the house; she wasn't ready for it to look so exactly the same. The junipers, the columns, the rattly upstairs window where you climbed out on the roof to smoke. Georgia touches the rear corner of their mother's car where the taillight is busted, the bumper buckled, the paint scraped with black streaks. Maggie pries a wedge of shattered red plastic free and holds it up. "Look at this. Even you . . ."

"Girls." There she is on the porch wearing a pink flowery apron. Gripping the railing, she steps heavily to the walk, holds her arms wide. Maggie rushes forward. "I was so worried about you." Their mother pulls her youngest close, laughing. Georgia waits until invited to step into her moth-

Jennifer Clements
Vinalhaven, ME

er's embrace.

"Come inside, you two; I need your help." She leads them to the kitchen and picks up a frozen burrito, lifts her glasses, and holds it close to her eyes. "What's that say?" Georgia pulls the burrito along with her mother's hand close enough to read the instructions aloud. They wrap the chilly white rolls and put them in the microwave. "A friend just told me about these," their mother says. "Easy solution to the problem of dinner."

The problem? Maggie remembers her mother's devotion to cooking—ragouts, fricassees, tetrazzinis—before anyone knew the words. "Every year, I made you do chicken dumplings for my birthday," she tells her mother. "Remember?"

"You two were my dumplings. Still are."

"I always wanted Spaghetti-Os." Georgia looks uncertain.

"Your father dreaded your birthday dinners, Georgia." A rueful smile. "The poor man could make me laugh back then."

After dinner, their mother pushes to her feet. Says she's worn out and would they mind tidying up. At the doorway, she turns back. "The car goes in tomorrow. Remind me, or I'll forget. Your father was proud of that car. He put the key so I'd find it in the fridge, the morning of my birthday. Okay, ancient history. You know where the towels are, Maggie. 'Night."

Georgia fills one sink with soapy water and finds her mother's yellow rubber gloves. Maggie closes the kitchen door. She grabs one of the empty wrappers from the counter. "Burritos!"

"What's wrong with burritos?"

"Our mother does not serve up packaged food from the freezer." She waves a dishtowel at the refrigerator. "Look at the mess of notes. Here's one for a dentist appointment three months ago." She wipes two fingers on the wall behind the stove. "Greasy."

Jennifer Clements
Vinalhaven, ME

"Our beautiful house. I remember the first time I brought Larry. He was . . ."

"This isn't about you, Georgia. This is about our mother."

"I didn't mean . . ."

"You always do this. For once, let's just focus on Mom. Is she even paying her bills? Is she thinking clearly? She said she'd forget to take the car in without us reminding her."

Georgia stands leaning forward, arms straight, yellow hands on either side of the sink, doesn't look up, doesn't speak. Then she snaps off the gloves, slaps them to the drainboard. "How many times have you been home in the past five years?"

Georgia's pissed.

"Who helps when Mom can't get a box down from the attic? Who's the one the hospital's going to call when she has a heart attack? It sure as hell isn't you, is it? You live in *New Mexico.*"

"You know I can't afford to live here. I talk to Mom on the phone every few days. Do you ever come over and just hang out? Or do you and your one-percent husband, who don't seem to have produced any kids, just sit over there in your big house and admire the sunset?" Maggie knows she's gone too far. She tries to backtrack. "The truth is, you can afford to lose our inheritance to some phone-scam person. I can't."

Georgia pushes off the counter and faces her sister. Her eyes are wet; her voice is loud. "How dare you. I have a happy life. I don't live in a trailer. You, on the other hand, are the spitting image of your loudmouthed, drunken, good-for-nothing, dead father." Georgia's eyes are on fire, but her fingers are at her lips.

Maggie gives Georgia a stiff little bow. It is, in fact, her father's gesture. For when things got beyond repair. She turns and leaves the kitchen, gets the spare house key from the hook where it's always been, and steps into the quiet night. The streetlights make a pathway of bright spots along the sidewalk, like at the end of the Jimmy Durante show

Jennifer Clements
Vinalhaven, ME

she'd only seen in YouTube videos, but that her father made part of bedtime. Goodnight Mrs. Calabash, wherever you are. It didn't mean a thing. It meant I love you no matter what.

She knows where she's going. She never travels without being prepared for this. Georgia will think she's doing what her father used to do and that she will come back hours from now, wasted. She walks past the centuries-old white steps that lead to the Sunday entrance of the Congregational Church. Around to the side is the lighted door to the basement, where a man leans against the wall smoking. He looks up. "Been here before?"

Relief, being with one who knows her before she's said a word. "Visitor. My home meeting's in New Mexico."

He puts out a hand. "Tom."

After the meeting, Maggie walks home. She turns the corner and sees their house, every window bright. There's Georgia on the couch. Perfect blond hair, gathered into some arrangement only she can achieve. Clothing that never wrinkles. Skin to match. Why isn't she home with Larry? Maggie knows why—because her sister can't leave an unfinished argument. She's always had trouble with that.

Georgia looks up when she hears the door. A glass in one hand, she tucks strands of hair behind her ear. Close up, Maggie sees that the perfect arrangement has come loose in some significant way. Georgia looks afraid. Her weakness makes Maggie want to hurt her; she's not proud of that. She sits in the chair across from her sister. Says "Relax. I went to a meeting."

Georgia sets the glass on the side-table.

"Don't worry about it; you can drink. I can't. The point is, what are we going to do about Mom?"

Georgia picks again at the fallen strands of hair. "What is it we need to do?"

"We'll tell her in the morning. That she's not driving any more."

"I suppose so."

Jennifer Clements
Vinalhaven, ME

A not very sincere but necessary hug allows Georgia to carry her glass to the kitchen sink, put on her coat, and go home to her husband. Maggie climbs the stairs to see if the towels are where she remembers.

***

It had gone well.

The next morning, after not much sleep, Maggie heard her mother in the kitchen. Georgia was due soon; she would be on time. That was one thing you could depend on Georgia to do right.

Downstairs, it looked like Mom was trying to make pancakes. There were packages of flour and sugar and blueberries on the counter, a jug of milk. She was doing pretty well. She had batter in a bowl, the frying pan on the stove.

When Georgia came through the door, their mother looked surprised. "Why didn't you tell me you were coming?" She had looked from one daughter to the other. Georgia was no help, going red and fussing with the collar of her trench coat. Maggie turned off the burner and guided her mother to a chair at the table. Her mother went between pleased, like maybe it was Christmas, and scared, like she knew bad news was coming. Maggie wished she could make it Christmas.

"We're worried about you, Mother" was the best she could do. She'd had all night to come up with something better. They asked about her medications and her bills and her checkbook. Did she know to hang up when somebody called and asked for her Social Security number? They asked if she knew who the president was, and she said of course she did; she just couldn't think of his name.

They finally told her that they knew she wasn't going to like this, but they thought it was best if she stopped driving, and where were her keys? She looked confused and then finally asked how she was supposed to get to work. Georgia asked what work was that, and their mother answered that

Jennifer Clements
Vinalhaven, ME

she works at Meals on Wheels. Maggie didn't know about it either, but volunteering is a good thing, so she asked if Georgia had time to drive her.

Their mother went for her coat and her purse. She got out her keys, undid the one for the car, and handed it to Maggie with a long look that Maggie couldn't quite get, and then asked her to please take the car to the bodyshop. No argument, no fuss. She had realized it's the right thing. Maggie hugged their mother, and she hugged her daughters, and it felt like a good conclusion to what could have been much worse.

End of the day, now, and Maggie is waiting for them both. Her mother left a message that she would take the bus, and Georgia called to say she would be here by five.

Maggie's been busy. Getting a ride from the bodyshop, she had a talk with the guy there whose mother also needs a little help. At home, she'd made a pot of coffee and set to work at the kitchen table. She called three different agencies about a helper who could come in and do some cleaning and some cooking and pay a few bills, keep an eye on things. A woman is coming tomorrow morning to interview. Maggie hopes Georgia can take off work, but if she can't, Maggie will manage. She knows her sister's never going to do this on her own, and a helper will buy time until they can find a safe place for Mom to live. Maggie also went online to find a local real estate company. The agent thought she could get out to take a look at the house before Maggie has to leave. Georgia's going to raise hell about selling the family house, but what else can they do? If Georgia wants to buy the house herself, well that's fine.

She hears a car door slam. Georgia comes in looking mad. "I can't believe how they say it's *women* who are the bad drivers." She drops a sack of groceries on the table. Bottles inside crash but don't break. "Dinner." She points out the window at her car. "Some idiot, in the parking lot; I clearly had the right-of-way." She throws her purse at the table. It

Jennifer Clements
Vinalhaven, ME

tips, and spills to the floor.

Maggie kneels beside her sister to help. "Are you hurt? Is your car bad?"

"I'm fine, and it's just a scrape, but it's going to mean calls to insurance companies and days with some horrible rented car and on and on. I do not have time for this." She sits on her heels and laughs unpleasantly. "Me and Mom."

"Hardly." She needs to tell Georgia now, before their mother gets home.

At first Georgia is polite as Maggie reports what she has accomplished. Soon, however, Georgia is on her feet, impatiently snatching jars and bottles and packages from the bag of groceries, not looking at her sister. She makes a bad job of folding the paper sack.

"What the hell do you think you're doing?" she finally shouts. "We talked about the car keys. We didn't talk about bringing in a babysitter. You have no right." She bangs a jar of olives on the table. "Damn it, Maggie!" She carries the mangled sack to the drawer where they go, stuffs it in, and slams the drawer.

Maggie hasn't yet mentioned selling the house. "I have as much right as you. Or are you the one who's supposed to make all the decisions?"

Hands in her pocket, Georgia looks to the ceiling and speaks as to a three-year-old. "I'm sure you are trying to help. But you don't live here. You don't understand."

Maggie knows that Georgia isn't capable of stopping an argument once it's going. She lays both hands flat on the table. "Let's start over. Can we do that?" Georgia says nothing. Maggie tries again. "What do you think we should do?"

Georgia glances at Maggie's hands, at her face. She sits. "I don't think we're at the caretaker stage."

Maggie says to look at the evidence. The house is a mess, Mom's eating frozen food, she doesn't know the name of the president, the car accident. As Maggie speaks, she doesn't look at Georgia. Instead she arranges the jars of olives and

Jennifer Clements
Vinalhaven, ME

artichoke hearts and tomato sauce into rows, like the setup for a game of culinary chess.
　Georgia is listening. She looks as if she could go either way. "Where is Mom, anyway?"
　"She said she'd get home on the bus." Maggie looks up at the clock, sees it's almost six.
　Georgia checks her watch. "Seems late."
　"She should have been here ages ago!"
　"Maggie, take it easy."
　"Don't tell me what to do. Maybe she's wandered off. Maybe she's walked in front of a bus. Maybe she's dead." She goes for the phone book and the phone. Pushes the jars and cans to one side to make room. "Police, hospitals. Are you calling, or am I?" Her voice breaks. She wipes at tears with her fingers.

***

　An adolescent with red high-top sneakers steers an unstable string of nested shopping carts from their pen towards the supermarket entrance, crashing, bouncing, barely missing a green Land Rover. Hilary admires the young man's energy and scans the lot for an approaching taxi. Having no car is extremely inconvenient. The bus routes are hopeless; she wasted a lot of time figuring that out. She could have borrowed Lucy's car at work, but Maggie would call the old-folks police, so the taxi will have to do.
　After the taxi, she'd called the house. She knows she's the last person on earth to have no cell phone. She got a busy signal, like every other time she's called this afternoon. She's late and knows the girls must be worrying, but until they get off the phone, they're not going to find out where she is. It's Maggie, fretting about something. Frankly this is why Hilary hasn't mentioned her job. Maggie would find it inappropriate for her elderly mother to have full-time employment. At least Maggie calls. One of her daughters is overwrought; the other

Jennifer Clements
Vinalhaven, ME

is all business. Hilary adores them both.

The reason she's late is that the meeting with the board ran long. The agency is having a problem with drivers being on time, and as executive director she had to persuade the board to review their policies for volunteer selection, which took forever; the board chair is better at talking than listening. The other reason she's late is that she decided to make chicken dumplings for dinner. The butcher with the good chicken is across town, and then she had to get back here to buy the rest of what she needs, all by taxi. And Georgia will feel slighted because there are no Spaghetti-O's. She wonders if they still make them.

She couldn't help but hear most of last night's discussion about her failing faculties. Why should she have to instantly remember the name of the president? She thought of it a minute later, but by then nobody cared. The house probably isn't as clean as it should be, but until this business with the board is settled, it will have to stay that way. She worries about the two of them, wishes they were kinder to each another. Was she too eager to work when they were little? Should she have shed poor Ronnie sooner? No point in fussing; that's Maggie's department. Maggie and her worries will go home in a few days, and then Hilary can dig out another set of keys and get back to normal.

The cab comes to a quick stop by the concrete bench where Hilary is sitting. She gets to her feet and begins gathering the plastic handles of her bags. The driver is talking on his phone, avoiding her until he's finished. His upper body jerks to music she can't quite hear. Music he is sure to extinguish when he sees how old she is.

Carol Leavitt Altieri
Madison, CT

Love, Let's Try Again

Years, escaping from my wounding path of pain
I recall blessed ones I have lost
and think of them all with Sunday-sermon reverence
that lengthens spring days with Easter lilies
unfailing visits to grave sites.
I did not think I'd have enough love
to give again.

Yet, I have a new companion,
His elixir of loyalty and warmth
infuses my blood stream.

He picks purple hyacinths places
them In a wooden wheel barrow
on the patio near the sliding glass door
fills it with soil and waters them.
He puts out water for the tree swallows
and purple martins that flit down
from his designer bird houses.

Painted turtles slip and slide in their rush to water.
The red-wing blackbirds call in the rise
above the snow that sinks further into the roots
of scarlet maples.
Wild blood root emerges from dead leaves
along the stonewalls like candles sheltered
from a soughing wind.
A great blue heron hitches a ride on a suite of thermals.

My body resonates in the hollows of my hips.
We go outside as dawn begins.
to see the canopy of stars
and touch the galaxy in many directions.

Camille Wade Maurice
Wrightstown, WI

Shifty Summer

Summer breezed in a few days ago
loaded with luggage as yet unpacked.
Before Spring could embrace her
she flitted south again
hopscotching and hobnobbing
with those already gifted.

Spring and I languish
at the table laid for her.
Vased lilacs hang their heads.
Spring shivers.
I sigh and rise to turn on the heat.

***

New Year's Resolution

No more big deals,
big pictures
or big ideas about making a big difference.
No more grand standing
or grandiose gestures of generosity.
I'm going for the smalls this year:
small steps, small change and small kindnesses.
Will trade big dreams for small hopes,
great expectations for little surprises.
Will open the door of myself
to the ordinaries...the small stuff
blessings are made of.

Jacinda Timmerman
Seagoville, TX

Who Would've Thought?

Who would've thought
God would come in the form of a helpless babe
From sin the whole world to save?

Gaze at that tender face;
Caress soft cheeks and hands.
Who would've thought these hands
Would one day bear the harshness of the cross?

Lift the slight head,
Too fragile to do so alone.
Who would've thought these small shoulders
Would bear the weight of the world?
Who would've thought these bright eyes
Would one day fill with sorrow that I might have a tomorrow?

Tiny feet stretched across slender arms.
Who would've thought they would one day be stretched upon
    a cross?
Tiny fingers once curled around a single digit.
Who would've thought they would writhe from an impaling
    nail?
Who would've thought such innocence
Would die for the evil sin of mankind?

Precious, precious babe.
Such precious sacrifice.
Who would've thought?

Jacinda Timmerman
Seagoville, TX

From swaddling clothes to grave clothes,
Only to lay them aside for a heavenly robe.
Angelic hands toss aside the stone.
You raise victorious!

The wonder of human life so delicate and intricate,
Fearfully and wonderfully made.
The wonder of the cross so harsh and unforgiving,
Yet through one death forgiveness and redemption available
    to all.

Who would've thought?
Yet You had it planned from the moment of man's fall.
With love You came.
With love You sacrificially gave.
In awe I stand, in wonder of it all.

***

P. C. Moorehead
North Lake, WI

The Ring

My ring is hammered,
hammered gold.

It wraps my finger,
though I am old.

My ring is hammered,
hammered gold.

It speaks of Life
and of growing old.

F. Thomas Crowley, Jr
Lincolnville, ME

Last Dawn

We miss the sun
It won't be back
The beach is empty
White with frost, seaweed black.

The clock of time
We missed our chance
to save our planet
no next time.

The sun never came up
so it couldn't go down.
We walked to town
everyone's gone.

Two foxes appeared
at our back door again
hungry, exhausted,
We took them in.

We shared the last
of the bread we baked
and the water we hauled
from a frozen lake.

The wind picked up
The power went out
Four of us huddled
under a blanket...peace-out.

John O'Kane
San Pedro, CA

Exhumation

"Has anybody heard what happened to Luke?" asks Mary, spurting free from a cluster of reunion cackle.

"You can find him out on Highway 61...at the cemetery," says John in a tone that suggests this should be common knowledge, even for those who escaped the hometown after high school.

"He passed on? What happened?"

"No, no, healthy as an ox, though his liver might be getting a little green by now!"

"What...what do you mean? Why would someone be at a cemetery if they didn't have to be?"

"Well, some of us have to make a living at this bump in the road, this truck stop to somewhere better," says Mark. "We all can't be models out in LA living the decadent life."

"Okay you guys, get on me for leaving this mausoleum! Thought reunions were supposed to be about good vibes?"

"Ours has to be about anything we can get. Small towns are about shortages, skeletons in the closets, bodies buried in mysterious places."

"Well, what do you mean that he has to make a living?"

"That's where he works," says John.

"Doing what?"

"Well, he works with the land, kind of a..."

"...you mean he's a...groundskeeper? I remember that he was into nature...went off once in a while into the hills, stayed away for days."

"Not exactly, he's kind of a manager, and...he certainly gets back to nature. Loves the earth you might say."

"That makes sense. He used to talk about getting a degree in management, maybe even going on and getting an MBA some day. He had a head for figures."

"Yeah, mostly yours!" says Mark. "He bombed out of

John O'Kane
San Pedro, CA

calc."

"And he came back from St. Augustine's after the first term," says John. "He couldn't adjust to the college life."

"Okay you guys...what's the joke?"

"No joke...he digs graves. Loves to work with his hands, and be outdoors. It's quiet, and he's mostly his own boss."

"You guys are putting me on! Luke was...wasn't he voted one of the most likely to succeed?"

"He is succeeding!" interjects Matthew, a hometowner who's been sort of eavesdropping from the fringe. His farm borders the northwest corner of the cemetery. "He's dug graves for nearly all of the families in the tri-county area. He's like a family doctor in a sense...just that he deals with all the babies at the other end when they're...well, he's a vital part of this community. What would we do without him?"

"Wow, you mean no one else would do it? I can't believe..."

"...in the age of high tech and all the upwardly-mobile maniacs who specialize," John inserts, "it's hard to get someone to do needed jobs at the low end."

"Funny! I guess I'm out of touch with the local job market. Why isn't he here...at the reunion?"

"Townies tend not to come," inserts Mark. "They drift off into their own circles and want nothing to do with traitors who've abandoned their homeland."

"You guys are here."

"We're the...exception that disproves the rule," says Matthew.

"What's that mean?"

"We just hang out when we can and...love everybody. The more contact we have with foreigners the more secure we feel."

"Hmmm! How did you get that special insight? How did you develop different than the rest of the townies?"

"The religious instruction we got stuck with us," says John. "We owe it to Father Paul. He encouraged us to be the

John O'Kane
San Pedro, CA

Lord's emissaries. That's how Luke sees himself too, doing the Lord's work kind of. But he has had to work a lot of hours lately because his helper up and quit and there's a backlog of vessels who need their final resting place, so he couldn't make it to the reunion. This is one occupation where the deadline is everything. Plus there's been a lot of new business. The farmers out by the Indian burial mounds are dropping like flies from some mystery virus and..."

"...come on you guys. You may have put your noses to the grindstone in religion class, but from what I remember you were also pretty big practical jokers in school."

"Come see for yourself," inserts Mark in a tone that's meant to dispel frivolity. "He doesn't exactly have office hours but maybe we can catch him at break."

"I suppose now you're going to say that he's on the graveyard shift!"

"You said it! He works at night anyway...likes this schedule because he can get more done in the dark and it's when people aren't around to bother him. And he gets his way since he has been at it for a long time. He rarely works overnight but because of all the extra work he'll..."

"...okay...okay, I get the picture!"

***

"See ya, Hayden. Go ahead and take off...think I can handle things for the next few hours," says Luke as he surveys the grounds beyond the edge of the cemetery. "Did you double check the mausoleum? Hate to see someone slip in there and damage the marble, like last month when those taggers marked up the archbishop's tomb."

"Or steal a body! Like that time when you were...taking a nap and they got one of the Redmond family in the old section. When the economy goes bad a member of the town's elite always gets grabbed."

"Those big headstones...they must think some still take

John O'Kane
San Pedro, CA

it with them like those people long ago who made mummies. But not too many believe in the afterlife these days."

"You've got Pluto in case..."

"...if he stays awake and doesn't get chased off by the raccoons!"

"I'll check if he's around before I leave."

"This is probably the safest place in town from things we can see. And the best place to get a glimpse of those we can't. If a spirit visits me I'll be...ready." He raises a thermos. "I brought a large one tonight."

Luke pulls the cart of tools from the shed and trundles it along the winding gravel path through the hills of the old section of the cemetery to the edge. The mix of the crunching gravel and the squeak of the cart's wheels, amplified from the relative quiet into the facsimile of an adenoidal lyric, is muzak to his ears. He's always ecstatic to break unhallowed ground, and is especially proud now that his business is expanding when so much of the economy is contracting. He feels responsible for the cemetery's progress and flashes on a state-of-the-art facility ten years down the road that's the envy of those in the larger cities around the area. He stops the cart and takes a long pull from his thermos, peering at the half moon through the overhanging branches of the nearby oak tree. His sips always put him in a solemn, reflective mood. He looks up and a gust of wind shakes the branches, followed by a grating surge of cricket chirps that suddenly cease when he steps on a mess of leaves. Are they bearing witness to his movements, his reflections? A blackbird dive-bombs from the top of the tree toward him, bee-lining across the moon. An owl dopplers an arcane message, as if weighing in on the changing noises. Then absolute stillness, a moment he loves when there are no people and all other life forms withdraw out of respect, offering a window for spirits to speak. Those who passed knew for however brief a moment whether another life exists. If only they could tell. He takes another pull from his thermos. Maybe the new family mem-

John O'Kane
San Pedro, CA

bers who will occupy this section will reveal themselves. Everything depends on him, and especially how he goes about preparing their accommodations.

He takes another pull from his thermos and the suffusion of alcohol laces a wisp of breezing fertilizer, giving him pause. The sensation enriches over the next several seconds and he feels someone nearby. He glances to his right and swivels abruptly clockwise but sees no one. Suddenly he wonders what the reunion was like. *Did his classmates have a good time? What did they talk about?* He snaps out of it and stumbles to the top of an incline, kneeling over a space that's only sparsely filled with grass, bowing in reverence. His lips move asynchronously for a minute or so and he turns to his left and upward toward the imposing gravestone in an expression of rueful surrender that contorts into cryptic vacancy. He back-steps down the slope, fixated on the stone, turning sharply for a visual sweep of the new space for resting souls. He opens his thermos and with his fingers as filter sprinkles wine on the space, spreading his efforts over the larger patch of ground. "It's ready for me," he whispers.

He wants to begin digging at the bottom near his tools but decides to start at the top, not far from the sparsely filled space, because it's illuminated by spots from the mausoleum. Due to the recent downpours the soil is remarkably soft, allowing him to make good time. Before he knows it he has a sizable hole, but he doesn't remember the process that got him this far. His mind is not really on the job. It's like he's working in a trance from the memory of having done this so many times before. Something else is on his mind, pressuring it in a sense, and the deeper he goes the more he feels it. And the more he feels it the more his awareness of the work fades.

A noise breaks his trance and he finds himself in a space that's unfamiliar. It's only roughly oblong. One side is longer and there's a cavity on the other of no more than a few feet that looks like the beginning of an effort to carve out a tun-

John O'Kane
San Pedro, CA

nel. He springs up out of the hole and inspects his creation, piqued by the shape, but realizes that he has to correct it and jumps back down, but feverishly continues to work the tunnel instead, now quite conscious of his work. After several minutes he hears what sounds like a piercing scream and creeps back to the opening. He looks up into what appears to be three faces peering over the lip and laughing. The paucity of light prevents him from making out who they are.

"Doing some creative gardening down there Brother Luke?" one of them asks. "You're hard to find. We've been calling, and wandering around looking for you, trying not to disturb the residents. Since you couldn't come to the reunion we brought a little bit of it to you."

Luke still can't make out their faces clearly but he recognizes the voice as John's.

"Come on up and meet an old friend. We'd come down there but might not be able to get out!" They all bust a gut. One of them falls to the ground and rolls over, nearly tumbling over the lip.

"You guys came at a bad time...I'm getting a new section ready." Luke doesn't smile. He feels nauseous, like someone who has been interrupted from deep meditation.

"It's reunion weekend...time to let it all..."

"...we see each other a lot and...there aren't that many in our class I haven't seen or even want to see."

"We brought someone you haven't seen for a long time and...maybe she'll cheer you up." Luke stretches to get a closer look but only sees his three gesticulating pals, and springs up over the lip. From atop he can see all three faces clearly, but no mystery guest. Mark and Matthew are both holding strings of plastic loops with a few beers in each.

"Here brother...loosen up." Mark hands Luke a beer.

"Don't touch the stuff...got my own refreshment." He raises the thermos appended to his dangling arm, opens it and takes a pull. "Is this friend an invisible spirit?"

"No, but she's...free!" They spread apart from each other,

John O'Kane
San Pedro, CA

bowing and gesturing at obtuse angles, and introduce the guest with a clown-like mien as they fall to the ground above the area where Luke was digging his tunnel.

Mary pops out from behind a tall gravestone and parades clumsily between two graves, moving toward them through the breeze-strewn streams of light, hidden and exposed, hidden and exposed, like a floating apparition that could very well pass for an invisible spirit, Luke reflects. As she gets closer he's almost sure he has never seen her before and peers at his frolicking pals for some kind of explanation, but they're oblivious.

"She looks expensive to me," Luke says as he joins the ground-sprawl, taking another pull on his thermos. She nears the group and as her form comes into relief it seems he recognizes her and he wills her to stop, seeing her moving toward him in slo-mo. In the several seconds it now takes her to slip behind him his expression blanches.

"She looks like a good investment!" cracks Matthew, popping another top to bliss.

"I'm working on my market value!" she retorts while crouching down behind him. She reaches around him and covers his eyes. He turns around slowly and she tries to give him a hug but he blocks the attempt with his arms and jumps up, hovering over the lip of the hole before backing slowly up the slope, eyeing the tall gravestone.

"Hey Mr. Sociable, this is one of our classmates...she's returned from the...oh, I almost blooped," says John, who rises awkwardly and shuffles gingerly up the slope.

"Maybe that's the point," she says. "He's more comfortable with the dearly departed." She steps a few feet up the slope. "What are we doing in a dark cemetery in the middle of the night? It's creepy! All this death...how can you take it?" She looks around and shivers.

Luke stares at an angle above her head, forcing the others to trace the imaginary point.

"What's wrong?" she asks, bringing his glance fleetingly

John O'Kane
San Pedro, CA

in line with hers. She moves a few more steps up the slope and he twists toward the gravestone but just as quickly twists back. He arcs around her, keeping his distance like she's carrying a contagious disease and swings down near the hole, looking down with a pained expression. But he begins to smirk, like he's spinning a yarn to himself in a private code that just went public. "Wrong? There's nothing I can…"

"You still with us brother?" asks Matthew, who's revealing flickers of sobriety.

"The room off the sacristy just before early mass and… the wine, spilt all over your dress on…the floor and…Father coming in to get me…starting the mass late…smelling my breath and your…seeing your…me falling down with the cruet tray in front of St. John of the Cross. I was the president of the altar boys. Cursed forever!"

"You…well, you…got a good memory for…but it didn't happen exactly like that…I never thought of it that much… our spirits and our bodies were joined that morning…we graduated to…"

"…let's get otta here," says John, "and take him with us. There's an all-nighter at the dunes…"

"…it was…awful! I couldn't get a letter for the seminary. Couldn't pray anymore."

"Didn't you…I mean did you ever talk to him and…well, try to explain or at…least get…"

"…there he is!" He looks up the slope and instantly charges toward the large gravestone like a soldier fevered in battle. "There he is!" Still pointing at it, he turns to look her directly in the eyes for the first time.

John bolts up the slope, followed by the others. They grab Luke and carry him back down, his arms and legs flailing. His thermos drops and rolls into the hole. He continues to try and free himself with his considerable physical strength, becoming an unwieldy package for these sauced spirits. They bowl over in a whirl of limbs, their synchronized surrender to

John O'Kane
San Pedro, CA

gravity collapsing the mound above the tunnel. Their bodies separate on the way down and pitch at varying angles from the pressure of the tumbling soil. The rupture releases the ground supporting the graves above them, bringing earthen forms and particles down like a storm-driven creek, subterranean minutiae now thrust above ground, exposed, stewing with chunks of marble and flower vases, a broken tomahawk. A femur floats by on the lava, followed by a chasuble, as he feels himself passing down with a current of damp dirt to a position of rest, wrapped in a warm shroud of primeval pungence. Dazed from the tumble, he lifts his partially-submerged arm and observes the new landscape of limbs planted in a perverse geometry and feverishly works to free himself from the muck. He retrieves a shard of wood lying nearby and furiously proceeds to excavate his friends.

***

Sylvia Little-Sweat
Wingate, NC

Garden

She stands taller than the garden
wall—supplicant and serene.
After winter's freeze a lone white
azalea blooms again this spring
to shelter now an angel's wings.
Early morning as rain gently
glazes her face, I meditate on the
the way it falls on your grave to
etch your name even darker in the
stone. I am adrift on a pitching
sea, for you always anchored me
amid life's mutability, its mutiny.

Byron von Rosenberg
House Springs, MO

The Old War Horse

The old war horse
hears the trumpet call
and once again he gathers
his strength to give his all.
He is alone aware
of the courage war requires
and despite its depth he knows
that he more quickly tires.
The younger horses watch
wondrous and blasé
thinking that the battle
is nothing more than play.
They don't yet fear the sound
of cannon fire and gun
or know that death can catch them
however fast they run.
"Nothing wrong with that,"
the war horse seems to think
for youth is an elixir
one has but once to drink.
He likes to stand beside them
for they are strong and brave
yet luck and circumstance will more
determine barn or grave.
The flags are all unfurled
and the battle lines are drawn.
The war horse feels the whip
and hurtles towards the dawn.
Farther now and faster
at the rising sun he races
stronger for the conquering

(continued)

Byron von Rosenberg
House Springs, MO

of every fear he faces.
And there are some who say
the war horse conquered death
for it was courage he inhaled
with each and every breath.

***

Peggy Trojan
Brule, WI

The Harness Bells

Four silver bells
on the ten inch piece
of cracked old leather
Mother saved
from the homestead
can whisk me back in time
more than a hundred years
Shake in sync
with the trot of horses
and I become my mother
tucked between her parents
in the sleigh
Frankie and Dickie
know the way home
nostrils blowing steam
in the cold night full of stars
Bundled in quilts and happiness
believing the whole world
is at peace

Goose River Anthology, 2017//97

Patrick T. Randolph
Lincoln, NE

Cancer Ward

We have come for my wife's
Fourth round of chemo; we hold hands,
Observe others in the waiting room.

A young boy bounces in with his mother;
Her tired eyes glance at us, then she calls
To her son, motioning with her hand to
Come and play beside her.

There, next to her seat, is an open box
Filled with bright-colored cars and trucks.

A sudden energy fills the room,
The magic of youth, the medicine of innocence—
The boy pushes the gloom of cancer away.

My wife smiles at his mother, I wink at the boy
And this little patient seems to cure the world
With his urge to make honking sounds and
Race cars around like it's just another November day.

***

How Gently Come Death and Disease

Life was so simple
Just a couple short months back—
My father—alive;

My dear, sweet wife cancer free—
The new life inside her—safe!

Helen Ackermann
Rothschild, WI

Rituals Mark Time

Black ice has disappeared
buffeted by winds from the northwest.
Marsh marigolds show their golden heads.
Perennials are free of protective leaves.
Rose bushes are uncovered.
Daffodils poke their heads upward.
Deer come to graze on day lilies; a shame.

Time to put in the dock.
Feet move more slowly, arms are not as strong.

Now a place to gather,
wet a line, launch a boat or kayak.
Space to watch sunsets
and listen to the chatter of
children in the water.

Winds become colder.
Boats and kayaks are pulled onto the shore.
Leaves fall on the water and sail away.
Frost covers the grass; at times even a flurry or two.

Time to take the dock out.
Knees seem stiffer.

Rituals mark time.

Sherry Ballou Hanson
Portland, OR

Hubble

Twenty-five years ago shuttle Discovery lifted
cradling the telescope, mother and child
to release in the vastness of space
this brave pioneer on a mission
but Hubble had a flaw;
its eyes to the universe blurred.

Like an earth child needing glasses
it tried to read the lessons
as it drifted among stars and planets
and other cosmic wonders passing by
until the mother returned
to repair the child, make it new again
and again until she got it right and said goodbye

and Hubble pushed on, moving parts
working in synchrony, glowing with pride
capturing images backward through time.

She circled coronal nebula's all-seeing eye and
traced the shattered remains of supernovae,
recorded far antennae galaxies, moons and rings
and the Marathon Valley of Mars.

Hubble pulses on, blinking, probing
the unknown until batteries run out,
lights go off and she comes full stop.

Kim Millick
Falmouth, ME

Mud Season Blues

It's early spring, according to the calendar. Snowmobilers have put their machines away for the year. Woods workers are bringing their equipment in to do annual maintenance. Mud-caked excavators, bulldozers, harvesters, skidders, and cranes parade through town on the way to their annual checkup. The massive metal hulks, hauled on low trailers, barrel past us. Heaven help anything that stands in their way. Caterpillar yellow or John Deere green barely peeks through a rough year of dirt and grime. Each scratch and dent on their metallic skin tells a story of a big boulder moved or a stately tree cut from its stand, and there are a lot of stories.

If their exteriors are any indication of what their motors and hydraulics look like, the maintenance folks will have their hands full. Other than the mechanics, the town is in an idle mode with little to do until the ice flows out, fishing season opens, and the tourists return.

It's bleak and raw most days with snow flurries changing to cold rain and sleet making us wonder if the sun will ever show again. The communal mood is almost as bleak. Men congregate at the coffee shop and women bring their yarn and quilting projects to the senior center for some social time. Both groups are hungry for a change to their days.

Ida, my forestry friend, is busy pouring over her aerial photographs for her spring tree planting projects. I'm finishing my quarterly warden report to give to the chief; how many "pinches" did I make with snowmobilers and ice fishermen? (Not enough.) How many sportsmen were stopped? (Lots.) How many miles did I travel? (Too many.) How many hours of formal training did I receive? (What's formal?)

The outside door to the office opens bringing in a fresh blast of cold air and a jovial, "Hey, how ya doing?" says some

Kim Millick
Falmouth, ME

male voice. "I need a fishing license for the year."

"Sure, Walter. I can help you with that," says Heidi, our clerk. "What's new?" she asks as she gets the paperwork ready.

"Funniest thing, the old girls at the senior center have hired themselves dancers."

"Dancers? What kind of dancers?" Heidi says, somewhat distracted.

"Not just any dancers," Walter says chuckling to himself. "They're coming from the casino down south. You know, Clydesdales or something."

"Chippendales?" Heidi asks, now very focused.

Ida and I push away from our desks and head for Walter. "Did we hear that right?" I ask Walter. "How do you know this?"

"My mother told me about the hussies at the senior center," Walter says. "They are trying to come up with fund raising ideas: Bake sales, craft fairs, you know the usual. Then ol' Bessie throws out the male dancer idea and all the old ladies got excited! Ma said, "There was no bringing them to their senses."

"So, when they coming?" Ida starts. "Who gets to go? It better not be just for seniors!" Ida rattles on to poor Walter.

"Heck if I know. Ma was so embarrassed; I didn't dare ask any more questions."

"Well, Bessie's my neighbor," I say. "We'll get the details from her."

A few hours later, Ida and I are knocking on Bessie's door with a bottle of wine between us. Bessie answers her door, sees the wine, and greets us, "Well girls, I like visitors who bring refreshments. Come on in!" Bessie's dressed in jeans and a nice cozy sweater that's hand-knit. She has a grandmotherly grin and warm charm to her. She's in good shape for her 70's, fetching wood for her stove and doing her own chores. We follow her inside as she digs into her kitchen drawer for a cork screw. I uncork the bottle while she reach-

Kim Millick
Falmouth, ME

es for three glasses.

"To what do I owe the visit, ladies?" she asks.

I pour the wine and hand Bessie and Ida both a glass. "Well, rumor has it you've got a fund raiser coming up," I say.

"We sure do!" she says as we clink our glasses together. "Best idea we've had in years! We've got Chippendale dancers coming to town and I can use your help. We only have three weeks to sell tickets and ask for donations to help the senior center."

"Well, anything we can do to help, as long as we're first in line to buy two tickets," Ida says.

"Good, I was hoping you two would help," Bessie replies. "The only place big enough to handle the crowd is the senior center's party room. It doesn't have a stage, but the school janitor says he's got some staging he can loan us. The senior girls are making bake goods for the evening, and Vessie's Market will get a couple kegs of beer at cost. We need to sell 150 tickets, which you girls can help with."

We brainstorm how we would blanket the area with ticket sales until the wine bottle is dry. Full of ideas and excitement, we leave with our assignments.

Ticket sales don't always render the same excitement everywhere. The local Baptist minister writes his opinion in the Eagle Lake Echo, "Loose Ladies Lack Moral Leashes." His parishioners do their best to discourage friends from buying tickets at local businesses and social circles. Discussions of the upcoming fun, excitement and curiosity do more to encourage sales than to dissuade them.

The following week, Bessie appears on the front page with her quote, "Beat the Mud Season Blues and help the senior center at the same time with a little fun entertainment." Pastor Dud is quoted as saying, "We don't need that kind of entertainment to rile up the fair ladies of Eagle Lake. We have *Bible Bingo, New Testament Tale-telling,* and *Saturday sing-a-longs* to entertain the idle."

Ticket sales soar.

Kim Millick
Falmouth, ME

On the day of the event, the senior center is buzzing with preparations. Glitzy decorations are brought in bags by slow-moving seniors. Something resembling a disco ball is hanging from the ceiling. Anticipation of the night is buzzing through the town like a hot wire around a horse corral.

Ida says she'll meet me there, encouraging me to show up at least a half hour early. *What does one wear to a male dance review being held in a senior center during mud season?* I opt for a skirt, leggings and knee high boots with a colorful sweater. My go-to outfit for going out.

The parking lot is jammed with cars overflowing into the church's lot. Finding a spot on the street a block down is fine. Music is blaring from the center like it's a night club. Gaggles of women are walking toward the building all a twitter. Julie, from the diner, is checking coats for a buck. "Hey Cat! Isn't this a hoot?"

"Hi Julie. Yeah, this is great!" I say. "You're gonna be able to see the show, right?"

"Of course; I get to escort the dancers from their dressing room when it's time. Ida and I helped Bessie earlier so we could get good seats!"

"Smart girls. Where's Ida now?"

"She's guarding their door so none of the patrons try to sneak a peek. I've never seen so much excitement!"

"Anything to help a good cause," I say. "I'm gonna work my way in, Julie. See you later."

Through the doors to the main room, beer glasses are full and ladies are jiving with the music. A group of middle-aged women are up on the makeshift stage dancing as if they've practiced their moves together. Young enough to be able to move, but old enough to have lost their shyness, they are entertaining the room of early on-lookers.

Long tables surround the stage with chairs perched side-by-side with gray-haired ladies occupying each one, shoulder-to-shoulder. Behind these front row seats are gals of all ages, anticipating a fun-filled night, smiling at one another,

Kim Millick
Falmouth, ME

laughing and swinging with the music. A couple of men are hanging back with Cliff, the senior center's audio man. I walk back to greet them.

"Cliff, you got everything under control?" I ask.

"So far, so good," he says. "Merle and Mort volunteered to come protect me in case these women get out of control."

"I thought I recognized you guys," I say. "You look different without your deputy uniforms on."

"You look kinda different out of uniform as well," Merle replies, shaking my hand.

From this vantage point, I see the disco ball is made of sequins glued to a large Styrofoam ball. Lights from below shine different colors as the light rotates different colored lens. "Hey, my parents lit their Christmas tree with something like that."

"Yep, mine too," replies Cliff. "Where do you think we got it?"

"Well, the old place, looks pretty good, Cliff," I say.

"Yep, I've never seen it this lively before. Thank our friend, Bessie, the organizer."

With that, the music dies down and Bessie takes the stage. "Is everyone having a good time?" she asks through the amplifiers. The crowd claps, whistles and cheers. "Thank you for coming and helping us raise money for the senior center of Eagle Lake!" More cheers. "It takes a community to make this happen and you know who you are, so let's not waste any more time patting ourselves on the back. Let's get to the reason we're here! Please welcome—Chip and Dale!"

From the shadows of the men's room come two bulky hunks dressed like Paul Bunyan look-a-likes, in red flannel shirts and tight fitting kevlar logger pants. The music throbs to "Let's Party" and the crowd goes crazy. The ol' girls in the front are bouncing, clapping, and smiling big smiles. The rest of the crowd is whistling and swaying to the music.

They're dressed just like my husband!" one hollers.

"No Christine, they're clean and smell good," her friend

Kim Millick
Falmouth, ME

hollers back.

The song doesn't end before another is queued up. No one seems to mind that it's one Chip, one Dale. Chip is blonde and very friendly. Dale is dark haired and mysterious looking. Each has a tan and no one cares where they got it. It just looks... fabulous.

Each dance number gets the crowd more energized and engaged with these handsome young men. Within a couple of songs, the dancers have taken a layer off to show six-packs that don't have pop-tops and biceps that only belong to men who work out—a lot. At intermission, a couple of cute, size two locals are talking with the boys while the rest of us grab another beer.

"I think that was a warm up!" I holler to Ida who is in the beer line.

A middle-aged lady next to me says, "Good, cause I'm warmed up."

The lights blink on and off, quieting the lines and encouraging everyone to find their spot. Before you know it, *Crazy Train* is queued by Cliff and the crowd responds. Chip and Dale do not disappoint their audience. They shimmy into a hard charging dance that delights the patrons as if they were preteens. The ladies are giddy with excitement and energy. Bessie is standing on her seat hollering, "Come to my train baby." The next set shows the genius of the tunes. It quiets down into a gyrating rhythm that generates lots of dollar bills into the tight shorts with suspenders of each dancer. The ol' girls in the front row pull ones and fives from their pockets to keep Mr. Dance in front of them. When they run out of money, the girls behind them come to the rescue with bills of their own.

By the time the last dance is held, everyone has spent their money and their energy. For the night, they've laughed and danced, forgetting they've had mud season blues. They bubble out of the center feeling absolutely lighthearted, unable to contain their laughter.

Kim Millick
Falmouth, ME

The event is the topic of conversation for months after. The senior center had the best fundraiser ever, the husbands and boyfriends think it ought to be an annual show, and the dancers leave, asking to be invited back anytime. The afterglow of the evening brightens the rest of mud season making it more tolerable with these playful memories.

***

Leonore Hildebrandt
Harrington, ME

Where the Lost Things Go

Her child is resting, tucked against her back
as she walks the great forest.

It is raining—their umbrella thrums a fitful rhythm,
trees rise to a monumental darkness.

A path amounts to more than cairns and sticks,
it is undeniable, like the mottled feathers

they find scattered on the gravel.
The eyes adjust to possibilities,

criss-crossing tales of malady and comfort.
She talks to the child of hunger, of dwellings underground.

A soggy doll someone left behind
stares into the ancient rain.

They return to their home, unharmed. The child
understands that puppets, too, have sorrows.

Gerald George
East Machias, ME

Thoughts in a Snowstorm

Last night the sky broke open,
coming down in slow, soft smidgeons,
unsullied whiteness covering
the dull ground.
Wild turkeys
in their dark garbling way
scratch under the icy trees
where the snow falls least,
then stand as if on stiffly frozen legs
huddling under their own feathers.

Black crows go flitting
through the bitter storm,
but other animals who do not fly
seek out the safety of their holes,
burrowing in the dirt.
All the world thus quits
its chasing ways, quiets down
as if to slumber under
a thick cloak until its white
disguise is gone.

How strange amidst this aching quiet
to think how many times
the wobbly circuit of our spinning rock
around the sun has brought on spring,
only to close it down again
until the next swing round-about.
All living beings on earth
grasp after the sun,
imagining that it will burn forever,
it's little wick eternal.

Gerald George
East Machias, ME

We make light of it,
bouncing out of our heated homes
in clothes heaped on for winter,
hurrying up the hillside to the top,
flopping on sleds that slash through piles of snow
with metal runners—down, down
down we fly!
—great flakes spinning out around us,
until, in a churning turn,
we stop at the hill's bottom.

Exhilaration's thrill—
the feeling that stimulates the limbs,
enlivens the mind,
comes from bursting with speed
past sanity's bounds;
or from running, swimming, driving, racing,
surpassing the last competitor,
over the goal posts, falling in a fit
of victorious revelry, shouting out
—"Yes, I am the best!"

Or writing a poem that wins a prize?
How is it that we show ourselves so limp,
parceling out portions of our time
to swap for a moment's what—exhilaration?
Go to the mountain top, then hop a sled,
and turning away from the burdens of the earth,
start sparking to the bottom—*tenir bon!*
As if we would not get there soon enough.
As if the clutch of turkeys, watching us,
would give a nit.

Gerald George
East Machias, ME

Indifference is a law of nature.
I make my tiny muse go all about,
up and down, forward, back, around
until I tire of the sound its marching makes,
realize that all of it goes nowhere,
and stop. Not with a double-barreled blast
of self surrender, but snorting—"This will sort
out just as well tomorrow." Then I throw
my coat on, take my unpretentious sled,
and head to the closest slope.

***

Elmae Passineau
Weston, WI

Engulfed in White

Twirling with the delight of children,
   snow covering our tennis shoes
   and the sun warming our bare arms,
   we marveled at the strangeness
   of winter in summer
   on an Alaskan glacier in June
The single-engine airplane had just landed
   and we alighted into a vast white and silent world,
   broken only by our own chatter
We ran and laughed and threw snowballs,
   while the pilot looked on indulgently—
   he'd seen it all before
We might have believed
   we were engulfed in cloud,
   but the silver plane sat *there*
   and we were not in it

Marilyn Weymouth Seguin
Akron, OH

Shaking off the Village

With writing we anchor the mind with the pen; with sitting, the breath; with walking we anchor our mind with the bottoms of our feet.
—Natalie Goldberg

One summer I reread much of Henry David Thoreau's writings. Like me, Thoreau enjoyed taking long walks to clear his mind and renew his spirit. Okay, okay. I also walk because the dog needs exercise and we both need to burn some calories. Maybe even skip a few meals. Thoreau doesn't make any mention of this in his essay.

Thoreau preferred walking in the woods. I like walking on the dirt road. He walked in a parabola—I walk in a straight line. Thoreau liked evening "saunters"—I prefer brisk morning exercise. However, Thoreau and I do share one thing in our walking habits. Like Thoreau, I try to focus on the moment when I walk, on what I'm seeing and hearing and smelling on the journey. I really do make an effort. Thoreau called it "shaking off the village."

Thoreau's essay on walking began as a lecture, delivered at the Concord Lyceum on April 23, 1851 and many other times after that. It evolved into the essay published in the *Atlantic Monthly* after his death in 1862. If you type Thoreau, Walking into a search engine, you will find the entire essay.

From Thoreau: "I am alarmed when it happens that I have walked a mile into the woods bodily, without getting there in spirit. In my afternoon walk, I would fain forget all my morning occupations, and my obligations to society. However, it sometimes happens that I cannot easily shake off the village. The thought of some work will run in my head, and I am not where my body is; I am out of my senses. In my walks I would fain return to my senses. What business have I in the woods, if I am thinking of something out of the

Marilyn Weymouth Seguin
Akron, OH

woods? I suspect myself, and cannot help a shudder, when I find myself so implicated even in what are called good works —for this may sometimes happen."

For me, "shaking off the village" is a difficult task, especially in the early summer when my head is still full of the work I need to do to settle in at my Maine camp on Little Sebago Lake. Early in the summer as I set forth on my walks, I make mental lists of what needs to be done, what groceries purchased, what maintenance issues resolved. Sometimes, I strike off with my iPod. But by the end of June, I am more likely to live in the moment as I walk. I listen for the bullfrogs when I approach the bog and I look for deer and moose tracks in the soft dirt on the side of the road. Sometimes on sunny days, I collect the glittering mica that breaks off the road rocks in wafers. Occasionally, I will strike off into the woods, following the snowmobile trails that criss cross the forest behind my camp.

I like to use a walking stick when I go into the woods. My friend Ed carved my favorite walking stick from a tree taken from our property on the lake. It is about five feet tall and an inch and a half in diameter. The top is carved into a bearded face, a wood sprite who scowls at me during our walks. The handgrip is wrapped in soft deerskin, laced on with a thin strip of rawhide. I take it into the woods in the event that some wild animal might try to attack the dog or me. Of course, that has never happened.

Once not long ago, I got disoriented while on a walk in the woods behind my camp. I was on a quest to find the old Prince family farmhouse that I was told was at the end of a path that led away from the lake. When I realized that I was lost, silence descended and I felt swallowed by the trees. My heart pounded in my panic. My fear heightened all my senses, and I looked around for something familiar, something I might recognize in the landscape that would set me on track once again. It was the lake that saved me. Suddenly I could hear a boat or maybe a jet ski on the lake in the distance. I

Marilyn Weymouth Seguin
Akron, OH

followed the sound. When I got home, I felt ridiculous. But I vowed never again to venture into the woods alone. For a while, fear kept me from that which I once enjoyed.

Then one day I left the dirt road and once again walked into the woods. Every day since then, I walked deeper into the woods until I was no longer afraid. Each day I went a bit farther, using the lake sounds as my guide. I never got lost again. All women need to go bravely into the woods. Getting lost can sometimes help you find yourself, and being lost is not the same as not knowing where you are.

From my reading:

There is nothing to be afraid of in the woods, except yourself. If you've got sense, you can keep out of trouble. If you haven't got sense, you'll get into trouble, here or anywhere else.
—Louise Dickenson Rich

***

Irene Zimmerman
Greenfield, WI

Dawn

In the gilded east,
trees hoist up the sun.
Song birds harvest breakfast
in the blue fields of sky,
while white hens fly
over the garden fence
to feast on sprouting greens.

A. McKinne Stires
Westport Island, ME

Without a Moon

I could jump out this window,
down to the lawn and
be swallowed by the night,
bare feet on damp grass.

In the light of the room
night seems black and empty,
but I know it's not.
I know what's going on out there.
I've been there,
sitting on worm-wet earth
listening to salamanders
stir the leaves.

I was there twenty years ago.
Got beggar's ticks on my sweater
crossing the beaver dam
without a moon to guide me.

Had to feel my way
across their mossy, tangled wall
with my toes, testing here,
and there,
like a daddy long legs
searching for a footing.

A. McKinne Stires
Westport Island, ME

Had to crawl backwards
through spruce boughs, so needles
wouldn't gouge my eyes.
Then I sat, very still, on a tree root,
somewhere near the Dunton graves,
                                  and listened,
                                            and listened, to
only a leaf, disturbed.

Twenty years, maybe more,
since I walked into the dark,
reviving my childhood delight
of walking to the woods
on the darkest nights.

Follow me through the window now,
and sit with me without the moon.
In the heart of darkness
hold the nightlife,
lightly in your mind,
a whisper of safety
when light brings
too much to see.

Steve Troyanovich
Florence, NJ

in the still fall of snow
Forever this sorrowful human face in eternity's window.
                        —Kenneth Patchen

there is no warmth anywhere
all is coldness…

there are no stars
no serenades of moonlight…

wars continue their ugly noise
political shams and slaves to madness…

no laughter no embracing
no faces blooming with rainbows…

there is only aloneness
this blanketing sadness…

all i want to do
is hold you…

Sharon Lask Munson
Eugene, OR

As a Matter of Luck

During the depth of the depression
my father won five hundred dollars
in the Irish Sweepstakes.

He, being a sensible man,
never gambled, lived prudently,
but couldn't say no to a good friend
selling tickets to finance hospitals.

The winning bounty
was a treasure to my parents.
They paid off their debts,
bought the friend a bottle of Jameson's,
banked the rest

keeping out a modest amount
for a quiet dinner
in a neighborhood café.

Amid Bing Crosby crooning
Pennies from Heaven
from a corner jukebox,
they sipped sweet red wine

toasted love, friendship,
and, of course, good fortune.

Pat Onion
Vienna, ME

The Call

After the meal they brought out the harp,
Passed it around the banquet table
So each guest could sing.
When Caedmon saw it coming
He ran miserable to the cattle shed
For he had no song.
And then an angel appeared to him, and told him:
"Caedmon!
Your song is holy!"

Loon calls rise off the lake
Finding a mate, staking territory.
Some say their song is the soul song of dead warriors.

All song is holy!
To know itself
Soul sings.

***

Sylvia Little-Sweat
Wingate, NC

Shells

Sea shells cast ashore
are the Deep's hieroglyphics
of Infinity.

Lloyd Ferriss
Richmond, ME

Those Blue Connecticut Hills

The summer of 1963 was the last time I lived at home with my parents and two brothers. Everything changed afterwards, as often happens when one moves into adulthood. I'm sure that's why I recall that long ago summer—and one event in particular—with such clarity.

Swimming was my favorite sport 54 years ago and, during that memorable summer, I had the perfect job for practicing my passion. I was a lifeguard at a pebble-strewn beach on the east side of Cold Spring Harbor on Long Island's north shore. Mornings and evenings I swam laps—back and forth, parallel to shore—as fast as I could propel my willing body. I'd do an Australian crawl for 100 yards, back stroke another 100, then breast stroke for a final 50. By August I felt wonderful and more than a little happy.

Vaulting onto my lifeguard stand one morning, I glanced north to the blue Connecticut hills six miles away. *I could swim that distance*, I thought. An instant later the inevitable follow-up hit my brain: I will swim to Connecticut.

So on my next day off I rented a rowboat, oars and a 10-horse-outboard. My 17-year-old brother, Bruce, and his high school friend, Barry, volunteered to row across Long Island Sound while I followed the boat. Thus the adventure began in morning fog as we motored out of Cold Spring Harbor to a north-pointing peninsula on the Long Island shore named (appropriately, I thought) Lloyd's Neck. I waded to waist-deep water and dove. Bruce navigated by compass until the fog lifted. During the first half hour, a curious porpoise followed me. Farther into the swim, I bumped into floating bags of garbage that I assumed to be remains of New York City trash dumped from barges into the Sound in the days before environmental awareness.

The sun shown warm, and Connecticut seemed slightly

Lloyd Ferriss
Richmond, ME

closer. When my goggles leaked, I threw them into the rowboat and swam on with no eye protection. As hours passed, salt water sloshing my unprotected eyes caused nearly unbearable pain. When it got to be too much, I swam to the rowboat's transom where Bruce poured fresh water over my upturned face.

"I remember you saying," Bruce recalls, "that you didn't want to touch the boat as that would have been an unfair rest. Besides a canteen of water, you brought along a repulsive raw egg concoction that you'd mixed up at home. You floated on your back while I pored this stuff down your throat."

Five hours after walking into Long Island Sound at Lloyd's Neck, the approximately six-mile crossing ended on a rock jetty in Stamford. I crawled onto the rocks shaking with fatigue. Bruce and Barry helped me into the rowboat for a short ride to a Stamford beach where I called home to inform my much-relieved mother I was still among the living.

Often turbulent Long Island Sound was pond-smooth for the north-south motor-powered ride back to Cold Spring Harbor. While returning boat and motor to the marina, Bruce and I decided to present my accomplishment to the local newspaper.

At *The Long Islander*, a now defunct weekly founded by Walt Whitman in 1838, a reporter took interest. I told him about the porpoise I briefly mistook for a shark. I described swimming among floating bags of garbage, and how my eyes pained during their long emersion in salt-water. The front page story that ran a few days later appeared beneath the headline, "Busman's Holiday—Local Lifeguard Swims to Connecticut." Curiously, few if any details I had relayed appeared in the account. Instead, the reporter compared me to the main character in Alan Sillitoe's 1959 short story, *The Loneliness of the Long-Distance Runner* (made into a movie in 1962).

I wasn't the least bit lonely swimming Long Island Sound.

Lloyd Ferriss
Richmond, ME

But the attention had some advantage. Beach patrons who read *The Long Islander* offered congratulations. Fellow lifeguards ribbed me mercilessly, yet with humor. I was happy during the final August days of my summer job. I had one semester to go before finishing college. Afterwards I planned to climb America's high peaks and do more epoch swims—financing this imagined vagabond life by writing first person adventure stories for travel magazines.

Those plans vanished a few months later when I impetuously married a woman I hardly knew. We moved to Maine and had two children, suffered a bad car crash, bought a house and eventually divorced.

I did find interesting work writing features for a Maine newspaper; a job much like the one held years earlier by the imaginative reporter who chronicled my swimming adventure. Today I'm remarried, retired and the author of two books.

Yet my thoughts drift back involuntarily to the summer of 1963. And I see in my mind's eye a ridge of Connecticut hills as they appeared from a lifeguard stand, and recall my youthful confidence that of course I could swim across Long Island Sound.

Robert Erickson
Round Pond, ME

A Desert Song

At sunrise the desert is a musty grey
The arid soil is a stone-hardened clay
The view shows staccatic cactus green
Then, suddenly it flowers like never seen
Petals flourish with colors of red and blue
Not just colors but brandishing every hue
Cactus huddles and scatters everywhere
Saguaro, Cholla, Barrel and Prickly Pear
As the sun sinks low and shadows grow long
We hear the coyotes sing their desert song

***

The Hummingbird Thrum

Have you ever heard a hummingbird hum?
Listen very closely to the "thrum-thrum-thrum"
Then watch that little stiletto-pointed beak
Dip and dip and dip; it's the sugar they seek
Then a twitch of the tail and off they go
To where; they are so fast I'll never know
Nor will I know where they come from
But I will listen again for the thrum-thrum-thrum

Paul G. Charbonneau
Rockport, ME

Immanence

If inside a block of marble or granite,
    Moses sits or David stands,
so too a blank page hides a universe of stars,
    waiting to be seen in daylight,
coming at us, extending their reach,
    leading us by the ear, wide-eyed,
toward sights and sounds divine.

This clean, white sweep of paper
    holds wonders deep and bright,
waiting for scribbled shadows
    to scratch its woven fibers
and draw droplets of starlight
    that bleed through the page,
silhouettes of lead now tongues of fire.

            ***

Viewpoint

I looked up
    at the sky,
then looked out
    into the universe
and saw
    sparks flying
    inside
    the mind of God.

Sylvia Little-Sweat
Wingate, NC

Genie

Summers on the farm
the Watkins' man
sold flavoring for cakes
salve for sores.
When he moved on
to neighbors' homes,
the vanilla amber
left for our kitchen shelf
shone like roasted chestnuts.

With stealth and glee
I would open one bottle
to free the genie
of snow-cream winter
and icing glaze—
the scented memory
of us huddled
by Grandma's
old wood stove
eating the numbing cold
Mother stirred from snow
Daddy skimmed at dark
from pasture posts
and windward drifts
while Sister held the pan.

Sylvia Little-Sweat
Wingate, NC

As the kettle hissed
and spewed
its dancing drops
we ate cups of winter
till we froze
breathed enough vanilla in
to last until summer's end
when candles on iced
cakes glowed
like winter coals.

***

Christopher Fahy
Thomaston, ME

December Deep

Driving home very late
past black forests and fields
in clear brittle cold
the children in back
bundled up to their ears
we arrive at our dooryard
get out to the sound of trees
cracking like gunshots in bitter wind
and we are so small under merciless
stars many dead, many dying
and think of how easily we could
be claimed by the vast frozen night
but we're only five paces away
from our unlocked door
and airtight stove
whose steady flame
will keep the universe at bay.

the late Joe Gray
Damariscotta, ME

The Fairy Diddle

At home in the spruce woods,
with bounding moves
across the forest floor.
He scampers up the tall spruce.
The rusty brown Fairy Diddle stops,
to chatter an alarm,
or is it just telling us,
"This is my woods."
He now scolds,
and is answered
by another nearby—the
chorus is on!
Back and forth.
One leaves, one remains.
chickaree, chickaree,
echoes through the still woods.
The challenge goes on again,
but no reply
The Fairy Diddle remains in charge
of his domain
Sitting on a low branch,
above his midden,
all the while
surveying his surroundings,
awaiting another challenge

Richard Manichello
Baltimore, MD

Mourning Becomes Spectacular

"No, I won't kiss him."
"He's your father."
"I never kissed him when he was alive, Aunt Lil!"
"But you two never…"
"And not now." I cut her off, brusquely, taking my voice down a few octaves to a whisper. "And that's final."
"It's just an old custom," she pleaded.
"Old or odd? The operative word, Aunt Lil?" I took a deep breath, then looked over at him.

We never saw things in a huggy, kissy kind-of-way. The hurt reflected in my aunt's look reminded me, uncannily at that moment, of the man lying in the coffin. They all had the same dimpled cheek muscles around the upper lip. Even dead, he seemed to be smirking, the knitted little dimple taunting me again.

My aunt backed away, her eyes wet and large with disappointment. She sat down in the front row of folding chairs along with the other three yard birds—my father's sisters—all perched like magpies. They looked fantastic, like a rock 'n' roll backup quartet. They were a striking ensemble, draped in the family colors: black on black. Diamonds and assorted stones flashed; heirlooms doled-out among the Dazzle Daughters by a generous mother. There was enough *bling* to blind an eagle. In mourning, they were spectacular.

The misery-and-grief circuit for them was a night out on the town. Entrances were like Paris runway; exits like a New Orleans jazz funeral. They were well-heeled and suited for sorrow, adding that special something to any vigil. Tight-lipped and taut-skinned, they looked like a cask of sparkling Greek olives. Their jet-black hair—pulled straight back, close to the head—they held a perfectly rehearsed pose whenever they gathered together. The Corpse-House tableau they pre-

Richard Manichello
Baltimore, MD

sented was a bronzed Rushmore of stoic ambivalence.

In a few hours they'd be all smiles and mirth working the room at the party. Yes, a party. The final night of a family wake warranted a big bash with lots of drink and homemade foods. It was custom and it would bring the bereavement to a satisfying close. With my dad lying dead—in a place called the living room, no less—the evening's guests would be having a feast throughout our old house. Visitors enjoyed wine, elaborate dishes, hors d'oeuvres, coffee and sweets. Friends sat for hours telling embarrassing stories, one after another, about everyone present and departed. Memorable moments in the account of my father's life, of course, burned brightly in tales remembered. A life diminishes and then extinguishes, only its story gets larger.

Out on the back porch, my Uncle Angelo sat in an old green Adirondack chair smoking a *Parodi di Nobili*, gazing off onto the long, fresh furrows of my father's meager vegetable garden. Moonlight cut the curving shadows of damp earth sharply. Leaves from the new pepper plants gleamed platinum white against the evening blackness. *Beneath that leafy camouflage*, I thought, *what succulents lie, what juicy, plump tomatoes–red and yellow and green–lettuces, tubers, squash and beans, eggplants, white fennel and red onion.* A silvery olive tree stood at one corner of the yard. The garden was a third of the size now as it was when I was a boy. Back then, my dad's unquestionable agrarian authority ruled, and I implemented his grand plan. The garden gave-forth in biblical proportions. Neighbors envied the bursting bounty of each year's crop. Baskets full of my father's luscious vegetables sat most August afternoons like French still life paintings on the doorsteps and porches along our street.

"He's not going to see his almighty tomatoes this year, kid," Angelo said, in the droll tones of the misanthrope. His stubble teeth gripped the stogie and he sucked deeply on the wine-dark rope of tobacco.

"Guess not, Uncle Ang," I agreed, hoping to halt the

Richard Manichello
Baltimore, MD

inevitable flow of sophistry.

Angelo's puffing and a few crickets in the grass filled the moment's stillness. In the near-silence I imagined myself once again humping full buckets of water, one in each hand, along the rows of my father's tomato plants. The buckets weighed heavily on my pre-adolescent arms and shoulders. Each tomato plant had to be watered individually, by-the-bucket, one to a plant. That's the way *his* father did it. I couldn't use the hose like modern Americans. I had to do it the ancient way—his way. I walked his perfectly tilled lines like a tightrope act. And he just sat on the porch, yelling.

—*You're spilling a lot of water, damn it! You're making double work!*

He had an old tin breadbox filled with ice and bottles of Ballantine beer next to his worn old chair, the green wooden chair with the one slat missing. His tattered straw hat and a brown beer bottle were all I could see over the porch railing from down in the garden between the tomato poles.

—*Watch! Don't step on those peppers, son. And mind the zucchini plants.*

I groaned. I cursed. Sweat ran into my eyes. I wished he would croak, right there in his wooden chair, tipping those cold Ballantines and smoking his Luckies.

***

"The witches are busting your chops, eh kid?" Angelo's voice broke through, bringing me back.

I turned and sat on the paint-chipped railing and watched my Uncle Angelo flick the solid round cigar ash to the floor beside the old green chair.

"Aunt Lil wanted me to kiss him…y'know?"

"There they go with that Old-Country crap again," Angelo shook his head. "Wait 'till you see what they've got planned for later."

"Tell me, please; I'm all ears."

Richard Manichello
Baltimore, MD

Angelo took the shriveled stogie, turned it sideways in his fingers and looked at it as if it were a fifty-dollar Cuban.

"Mourners," he said, flatly.

"You've got to be kidding me!" I watched the thick, white smoke strand from his cigar rise.

"Professional mourners," he said. "A bunch of Sicilian women who got nothing better to do than come and cry at somebody else's wake."

"Seriously?"

"Old custom, kid. They whip everybody up into a crying frenzy, especially the women. Supposed to be good for you, see, supposed to help your suffering. Supposed to be what they call, cathartic."

"I'll be damned," I smiled.

"Found 'em on the Internet," Angelo said with a sarcastic leer. He puffed on the dark stogie again. "We Weeps-dot-com," he said, dryly.

I stifled a laugh. Angelo didn't smile. He placed the cigar butt back between his teeth and sent a plume of the white pungent smoke out into the cool night air.

"Three sisters and a couple of cousins from over in Southside," he said. "They do some catering too. Pick up a nice piece of change, this bunch of wailers." Then, Angelo tagged-on his disparaging suffix, the final assessment he attached to all such folly.

"Some shit. Some shit, I tell you."

"They've got to hire people to cry for him," I said.

"Hard. He was hard, kid," Angelo replied.

"Mean. He was mean, Uncle Ang," I insisted. And at that moment I was beginning to feel a twinge of sadness at the loss of him, a measure of the profound remorse that is supposed to accompany the occasion. "He thought I was his mule, Unc, he drove me like one."

"Discipline is another form of love, kid," my uncle said, very matter-of-factly, as if it were the title of some recently discovered, long-lost gospel.

Richard Manichello
Baltimore, MD

The words could have come from anyone of their generation, chiseled into a stone arch that all of them once passed beneath when they entered this country. But love and hate only get more complicated as you get older, and my enmity seemed to grow exponentially. Then he died. And everything I felt would just die with him, interred someplace forever.

***

At nine-thirty that evening the professional criers took center stage. And they did not disappoint. It was a fantastic performance of breast-beating, chanting, keening howls, and shrill Sicilian braying. The show in our living room could only be compared to the best Greek tragedy. The people present relished the intensified woe. My Uncle Angelo sat in the back row watching as the Southsiders convulsed and gyrated around the room in front of my father's bier like *Bacchae* women. Angelo's tearless, sour expression, his eye-rolling silence and labored body language conveyed a familiar old refrain—some shit.

I could not weep nor grieve, outwardly, save for some funny thing that was happening with my cheek muscles around my upper lip. Within, I was a torrent of fear and gripping anguish. Apparently, the professional mourners had helped me wail against a wall of my bitterness and resentment. Perhaps it softened, just a bit, the hard memories I harbored.

Mourning increased by theatrics, lamentations hyped-up for a better catharsis—things to soothe the living. Loss, once established, wanted only for a glimmer of recognition. I could do that. I could give him that much. Bereavement took the same shape no matter what you were secretly feeling. And somehow, love and sorrow, even when camouflaged, intermingled there in our old living room and finally found expression.

Robert B. Moreland
Pleasant Prairie, WI

Hummingbirds

In the state park visitor hall
he lays, wings extended, tail fanned.
Valiantly he struggles, alive.
We wait in awe of his beauty.

Was he a king? Did he live here
with his only mate and enjoy
sweet nectar of wildflowers spread
across the kettle moraine hills?

The guide scoops him gently on paper,
we take him out, hoping he'll fly
but death is upon him. He heaves
a sigh, squinting liquid black eyes.

Emerald green train on his back,
I lay him with reverence near
a sunlit patch of reeds, praying
he will revive. But he does not.

What of his mate? She had struck the
east window lost in morning's glint.
Her neck broken, she wears the same
emerald green, delicate back.

Life's tragic brevity is lost
when we miss the subtlety of
the Creator's hand as He pens
fine "I love you" notes to us all.

1800 Cape

She seems at peace on the hill,
poised like a martyred saint on a pyre,
surrounded by woods,
bound with venous tendrils
under clapboards and door sill,
ants gnawing at her soul.

Another year, another snow
drifting in the opened doorway,
may tip the balance,
her perseverance spent.
The elegance she had is there
under plaster, fallen,
on cherry newel and winding stair.

The fields and farms have faded.
Her usefulness has waned.
With no builder's kin to mend her,
in thirty years,
her shine has peeled away.

Yet underneath her gray
and flaking skin,
lies a weakly beating heart
pumping pathos
and promise
through a savior's dreams.

Irene Zimmerman
Greenfield, WI

A Family Story

Aunt Katie:
It gets so lonely here in the nursing home.
I called my niece Helen to come this afternoon.
Yes, dear, it's really urgent, I said. *No, it can't wait
till Sunday.* She probably guessed that I just want to talk.
I have so many family stories to tell her
and I'm the only one still alive who knows them.
I didn't call my daughter. She's always too busy.
And besides, she never really listens. She complains,
Mom, I've heard that old story a hundred times already.
Helen isn't like that. She sits there quietly and listens
and smiles. I hope I don't forget any details this time.
It's getting harder to remember.

Niece Helen:
Aunt Katie called and asked me to come. She said
it's urgent, but I know she just wants to talk.
She's a dear old lady, but honest when she launches
into one of her endless stories with her usual
Did I ever tell you...? I'm tempted just once to say,
*Yes, Auntie, you've told me that story, maybe
a hundred times.* But of course I won't do that.
I'll sit there and smile while I mentally finish
my grocery list and hope there'll be time enough
to shop. It's hard to get away. When I finally stand up
to go, she'll beg me to stay a while longer and thank me
so profusely that I'll promise to visit her again on Sunday.

***

Irene Zimmerman
Greenfield, WI

Epilogue:
I miss her. And her stories! I wish I'd really listened.
She knew all the answers to the questions
I didn't think to ask. And now there's no one.

***

Ensign Son

He phoned her from the ship after a day
on shore leave. *Not enough time to tour Hong Kong.
You're going to love what I bought you, Mom. . . .
No, you'll have to wait till Christmas.* He didn't
feel so good, he said at the end. *Chinese food . . .*

She was already in bed when she heard
a car slow down and pull into the driveway.
She grabbed her robe and went to the door.
Through the peephole she saw two men
in navy uniform, waiting.

The words stung like acid on her tongue
as she repeated them, listening intently
to each monosyllable, trying to comprehend:
They found him dead in bed. When finally,
she understood the words, she informed the officers:

*You've made a mistake. My son's fine.
He called this afternoon.* She saw them glance
at each other, noticed their discomfort and added,
kindly: *You've come to the wrong house.
Easy to do in the dark on a country road.*

Goose River Anthology, 2017//135

Karen E. Wagner
Ashland, MA

Graveyard of Lost Moments

Something about the turning
of the seasons touches my soul.
Passing of years measured in the march

of weathered days swept by wind,
rain, a little sun and always the
humidity of this maritime region,

letting my body know time is
rushing by in step with the
lapping of waves between the rocks.

Better scurry to use these hours well lest they slip
from my fingers—gone to the graveyard
of lost moments and unworthy dreams.

Minutes are calling my name,
no room for hesitation as I
race to be included in the future.

***

Sylvia Little-Sweat
Wingate, NC

Iris

Purple silk standards
unfurl in the breeze—herald
the passing of Spring.

John T. Hagan
Springboro, OH

A Sister

Growing up the youngest boy in a three-boy, no-sister family, I, like those who had an imaginary friend, had an imaginary sister. I am now, however, rather discomfited that my fantasy sibling was not just the product of my early childhood but a flight-of-fancy that lingered into my early high school years. Since my two brothers were significantly older than I and since my home was located well beyond the nuclear neighborhood of my Catholic grade school, I was often left to my own imaginative devices on long summer days. When I was eight years old, my mother went to work full-time at the county auto-title bureau to supplement my father's very modest income, and I was often home alone during the daylight hours, our fifties and sixties neighborhood being under the plenary protection of busybodies and surrogate mothers. In early childhood, I would, of course, summon saddle pals like Roy Rogers and Hopalong Cassidy when the need arose, and they served me well when western adventure was the whimsy *du jour*. On other occasions, the basketball court in the alley behind our garage provided the setting for last-second heroics I performed in the assumed identities of college basketball stars. Faking the defender guarding me, I would pull up and launch the shot "from downtown," which I often needed multiple attempts to make. No matter, the crowd was equally jubilant even on my tenth or eleventh attempt. Those halcyon years of the early fifties-to-sixties were fecund times for kids' imaginary worlds. The days of computer games and lurid videos, which in my opinion have denied kids the skills to entertain themselves, would have been pure science fiction to us products of the Eisenhower Era.

In time, my imagination carried me to thoughts of how an older sister might enrich my male-dominated life, and in my

John T. Hagan
Springboro, OH

mind's eye I began to embody her in various personalities.

My "sister" had a number of identities or images drawn from a newspaper comic strip, a television series, and a real-life experience. Somewhere between the ages of eleven to thirteen, I began to fixate on one of the Jackson Twins as my imaginary sister (although I'm not sure which, Jill or Jan). The Jacksons, gorgeous and extroverted, were comic-strip products of the creative illustrator, Dick Brooks. Although they had a pesky younger brother, Junior, I was able to dislodge him in my mind and insert myself into situations that allowed me to interact with one of the twins as my older sister. She would sometimes elude my attempts to converse with her, but if my fantasies were on overdrive, I could deliver her into comforting moments of sisterly affection, made even more meaningful because of her teenage beauty, effervescence, and charm.

Probably around ninth grade, the quintessential girl-next-door became the sister of my dreams. She was none other than Betty Anderson of the fifties-sixties mainstay of television, *Father Knows Best.* Betty, played by Elinor Donahue, was not just a comic-strip illustration but real flesh and blood, with physical qualities and an intoxicating voice and personality. I think I resented Bud, her brother, played by Billy Gray, because Betty was my sister, not his. Betty was everything I desired in a sister: comical but not silly, loving but not mushy, puckish but not mean, studious but not nerdy, gorgeous but not vain, popular but not haughty, and engaging but not suffocating. My pillow became Betty at night, and she would often counsel me in regard to my fourteen-year-old issues, or she would spoof me out of my doldrums with her wit and laughter. I truly loved her!

Betty would tell me how to talk to girls or how to call them for a date, although as a student in an all-male high school, I rarely had the opportunity or courage to do either. As I consider my fanciful relationship with Betty Anderson, I

John T. Hagan
Springboro, OH

now wonder whether I imagined her as a sister only as subterfuge for my affections for her as an older girlfriend. Clearly, my interest in any episode of *Father Knows Best* ebbed and flowed in concert with the scenes involving the fetching, red-haired Elinor Donahue. No doubt, my fixation on Betty was shared by legions of male viewers. To this day, the mere mention of Elinor Donahue will educe the fondest memories of that willowy whirling dervish whom Jim Anderson called "Princess."

By my sophomore year in high school, I should have progressed beyond imagined relationships and pillow conversations, and, but for another set of identical twins, I had. What made my attraction to this real-life set of twins positively ludicrous is the fact that I do not recall and may never have known their names. For me, these stunning twins were clearly an admixture of sister fantasy and romantic desire. While typically alternating with each other during after-school and summertime shifts, they were sometimes assigned together, working the soda fountain at a very popular neighborhood drug store.

The Twins, as I shall name them, were seniors at a nearby public high school when I was a sophomore at a downtown Catholic high school. I first saw them in the summer before my sophomore year when they were working side-by-side during an ice-cream-eating contest, for which I had neglected to submit the pre-contest entry form and fee. I attended the event, however, because word had spread that a fullback classmate of mine was a heavy favorite to carry the day (if not the ball). While many spectators packed the space behind the competitors, cheering them to voracious consumption, I was nearly hypnotized by the heavenly twins serving the ice cream. Tanned-skinned and pony-tailed brunettes with sinewy arms exposed by sleeveless white blouses, these 5'8" mirror-image beauties worked the counter frenetically in their snug Levi's, serving vanilla-faced gluttons with each additional scoop.

John T. Hagan
Springboro, OH

The Twins became my playful older sisters who alternately teased and bolstered me during a somnolence induced by the hum of trolleys that powered the transit buses taking me home from high school. Often, I'd assuage the blunders and chagrins of a bad school day in a reverie imbued with my sister twins who would laugh me out of my crestfallen state or offer just the right succor for my damaged psyche.

Today, I am a bit curious as to how a skilled psychologist would characterize my imagined sisters. Since my family life was bereft of females other than a stolid mother whose long workdays left little in the way of womanly influence, I suspect that psychoanalysis might reveal that I pined for a feminine presence that was all but absent from my daily life. Additionally, this same analysis could show that my imaginary sisters filled a social void resulting from my sparse contact with girls. I was, in fact, almost terrified of girls, and throughout my high-school years, asking one to a dance, a movie, or an event was tantamount to the most fearsome of human endeavors. A telephone call asking a girl to a dance required days of courage building, hours of rehearsals, and multiple face-saving responses to hypothetical rejections.

Perhaps I'll never know whether my imaginary sisters were some kind of psychological aberration or just a need filled by fabrications, but even now, I still recall wistfully how these simulated siblings provided the companionship I needed to navigate the vicissitudes of junior high and high school.

Roselyn Stewart
Brookfield, WI

Capricious Mind

Lost in a daydream
Now happy
Now sad
Painful memories
Always alone
Anxious
Unhappy
Talkative
Outspoken
Escape from myself
Books my cover
Unhappy adulthood
Three children
Divorce
My mind races
Try to gear down
Can't find "Neutral"
Plunge into depression
Feel like I've drowned
My illness apparent
Diagnoses bi polar
Medication to follow
Baffling disorder
Creativity my savior
It's been there all along
Impressionable
Sensitive
Emotions strong
Pills finally work
I'm stable
Daylight in sight
I'm able

Edie Schmoll
Menifee, CA

Prelude

Now I wait for you; oh but call me
                and I will come—
As the great ocean tide
                tumbles surf on the rocks,
As the mercury moonlight
                slides glow on the river,
As the whispering winds
                commune with the clouds . . .
Long am I patient; but hear my need,
                and let me love you—
As soft-falling rain
                pads over the earth,
As sunrays discover
                a gentle new dawn,
As the powers above
                send the beauteous snow . . .

                        ***

P. C. Moorehead
North Lake, WI

Changing

The evening clears.
The stars light.
I breathe.

The darkness lifts.
The season changes.
I live.

Sandy Conlon
Steamboat Springs, CO

The Quilters

It was a loving conspiracy
By the Ladies Auxiliary
Making patchwork quilts
From the scraps of other people's lives
And they gave them all away

Like goddesses in some ancient rite
They plied their trade late at night
While men went off to war
And children slept
The peace was kept

They hummed and sewed
Pieces of cloth stitched with care
While favored hymns filled the air
And each colorful square
Became a kind of prayer

For occasions and celebrations
In need of blessing
To cheer an ailing child,
Comfort a wounded heart,
Console a dying friend
Or caress a newborn
      with the gift of worldly love.

Paul McFarland
Lincolnville, ME

Service Station—Closed

One Sunday while out on a drive
And thanking God to be alive,
I spied among a stand of birch
A lonely, rundown, country church.

I stopped beside that gravel road
And up a grown-up path I strode,
Intent to find what was in store
Behind that church's oaken door.

I thought it just a trifle odd
To find this little House of God,
That Sunday morning, warm and splendid,
So closed up and unattended.

As on that door I gently pried,
On squeaky hinge it opened wide.
A portal to a time where trod
A people more in touch with God.

And as I entered that old shrine
Whose maintenance was in decline,
I felt the presence of those souls
Who used to fill those Christian roles.

And years ago some congregation
At that rural byway station
Heard about divine reward
From some young agent of the Lord.

Paul McFarland
Lincolnville, ME

But gathered dust upon the pews
Was one of many silent clues
That hinted of a fruitless search
For hungry souls to fill this church.

An echo from some ancient prayer
Came tumbling down a creaky stair
That led to where a rustic choir
Once filled that church with heav'nly fire.

And as I listened, I heard soft
And plaintive tunes come from that loft,
And they brought back to me a time
When this old church was in its prime.

The altar stood in disrepair,
While shafts of sunlight filled the air
That filtered through those colored panes
To shed some light on God's remains.

And as I stood there in the gloom
Of Heaven's country anteroom,
I wondered if we could restore
God's House to what it was before.

And as I turned to take my leave,
I wiped a tear upon my sleeve.
It seemed a shame that there should be
But two souls here—just God and me.

the late Edward O. Barsalou
Kittery Point, ME

The Little Things That Warmed My Soul

I remember the little things that warm my soul.
Having a house full of young kids did it at times.
The little things made it all worthwhile.
I remember when the mail lady delivered the Sears'
    Wish Book.
True, the kids jumped higher then I did.
But I liked the pictures too.
The entrancing aroma of a Thanksgiving turkey cooking,
The smell of an applewood fire.
The gentle tapping of rain on the roof during a summer
    shower.
Even a lonesome feeling when sleet hit the windows,
    it warmed me.
The warm feeling that comes over me when we're all together.
My grandchildren.
My truck, when it's cleaned and polished.
The thought of a double Martini with three big olives,
And you by my side with a glass of French Chardonnay.
The simple things keep me warm inside.
The simple things keep us loving one another.
I still feel warm when the wish book comes.
No matter how little a thing it has become.
Thinking of Christmas in April, that warms me too.

Celine Rose Mariotti
Shelton, CT

Things I Remember About Nonie and Grandpa

The aroma of Italian coffee brewing on a Sunday afternoon. We'd all go downstairs to my grandma's and have coffee and Italian pastry with Nonie, Grandpa and Uncle Dominic. I loved the chocolate éclair and the Italian butter cookies. Nonie always put more milk than coffee in my cup and my sister Margaret's cup because we were so young. I can still see the blue and white flowered demi-tasse cups. My mom and dad, my Uncle Dominic, and my grandparents would all tell stories about people they knew and things that had happened. A lot of times Grandpa would tell funny stories and he'd make us all laugh.

I always remember the story that Grandpa told about how he and his friends sewed the hems of the ladies dresses. When he was young, back in the early 1900's, ladies dresses were long. He and his friends had gone to church and when the ladies were kneeling down, he and his friends sewed the hems of their dresses so when the ladies got up, they were all stuck together and they couldn't walk. My grandfather and his friends thought it was funny but they were young boys at the time. Anyway, we all laughed about it.

I can remember sitting on the back porch in the summertime talking with Grandpa. He always wore a Kelly and his light brown sweater. Grandpa wore glasses and he walked with two canes because he had no knee caps. He'd tell me stories of his life when he was a young boy in Italy. One of the funniest stories he told me is that the chicken only has one hole—it can't do peepee, it only does poop! He also told me that when they take the beans out of the chicken, that's when it grows as a capon. For all of us who are Italian, we know how delicious and succulent a capon is. The only other nationality that cooks capon are the French. There's a reason why the best food in the world is Italian and French. We

Celine Rose Mariotti
Shelton, CT

know and understand food and we enjoy it!

    Speaking of food, my grandmother made her own homemade raviolis, gnocchi and lasagna. She would make her own dough and put all the round cakes of dough on a sheet on my uncle's bed. When the dough would rise, she would take one dough pie at a time and bring it to the kitchen table where she would knead the dough. Once she had it all spread out, that's when my sister Margaret and I and my grandfather would cut the squares to make the raviolis and then we'd add the ricotta cheese. My grandmother would put on a big pot of boiling water and start cooking the raviolis while she also made the sauce. When we were all done, whatever ricotta cheese was leftover, she would put it in a dish for Maragaret and I to eat. So many wonderful memories of Nonie and Grandpa.

    A lot of times during the summer months, my sister and I would accompany my grandmother downtown to go grocery shopping. Her first stop was always the bakery and she'd always get us one Italian butter cookie each to eat before we headed to the Fulton's Market where Nonie would get her meat and fruit and other things she needed. She always bought us a box of Animal Crackers or a box of Jacks. The butchers at the Fulton's Market all knew my grandma and they'd always have a conversation with her. After we finished at the Fulton's Market we'd go across the street to the old A&P and my grandma would buy the Eight O'Clock Coffee for my grandfather. It was his favorite coffee. She'd always give us each a dime to put in those machines where you get a little toy. Then our last stop would be either the drugstore to pick up medicine for my grandpa or we'd go to the Five and Ten and a lot of times my grandma would buy us each a toy there. I always remember when she bought me the toy guitar. I always loved the guitar and I have been playing since I was a nine years old. I play acoustic guitar, electric guitar, classical guitar, bass guitar and the banjo. So many wonderful memories of Nonie and grandpa.

Celine Rose Mariotti
Shelton, CT

When I would come home from kindergarten, my grandfather would make me what the Italians call panne cotto. It is bread mixed up with leftovers from yesterday's dinner and he would make a soup out of it. It was so delicious. I also remember how Grandpa would peel an apple or orange, he would peel it so it all came off in one big round strip. How he did it I'll never know. But he was amazing to watch.

Grandpa made his own wine. He had all the instructions for making his wine written in his special notebook but he knew it all by heart. He would stand on the cellar floor holding onto his two canes to keep him upright and tell my dad and uncle what to do, step by step. I still remember the old wine press and I can still see my dad and uncle turning that wine press. My grandpa had two big barrels where he fermented the wine. He even made Vermouth. My sister and I were very young and we would sit on the cellar steps and watch everything. Years later, Margaret and I took a trip out to San Francisco and we went to Napa Valley. Seeing the vineyards and wine presses brought back memories of Grandpa. He was a special person.

I learned to make the Palm Crosses for Palm Sunday by watching my grandfather. He taught me how to do it and I still make them today every Palm Sunday.

After my grandpa passed away, a lot of times when my Uncle Dominic went to New York City for the day, I would go downstairs and have coffee and cake with Nonie and we'd sit and talk for awhile. I always treasure those special moments.

Even though it has been many years now since they both passed away, somehow they're always with me and I think about them often. They were two special people. So many wonderful memories.

Steve Troyanovich
Florence, NJ

night blankets the stars
Time is a bandage that leaks
Glimpses of memories and touch
—John Trudell

do you want to dance? she asked
no i replied

she said *i know you don't want to dance*
with me because i'm an indian

feeling the history of hurt haunting her eyes
will she believe me if i tell her
she is so lovely
...but i can't dance

later...**three dog night**
cascading from inside the open door:
mama told me (not to come)...

holding each other...under that night
that night blanketing the stars

A. McKinne Stires
Westport Island, ME

Homeless

Head tilted, tired of life,
she swayed in rhythms,
like a slave wailing
somber spirituals,
all hope of Africa
dissolved forever.
"Jesus in Heaven, please take me home.
I want to see my mother again."
Over and over she moaned,

her large, sad body,
welded into a corner
between two buildings,
baking in the afternoon sun,
dress flowing to the sidewalk
like a torrent of tears,
her magnificent black face
squeezed into furrows,
eyes shut tight against the world,

tired of platitudes,
and rusted promises,
tired of the flow of the guiltless crowd,
weary of people with city-hard senses,
and weary of being alone,
"I have no home," she cried,
with the breath of a sparrow,
"Help me, Jesus, help me."

Jeffry Knuckles
Phippsburg, ME

Dreams While aboard the Train from Parma

Pale golden walls these windows pass
Where monks still kneel at silent mass
And pray for men who left a trade
To join a papal-paid crusade.

Bright rails now mark their paths well-trod
Those sandled feet that marched for God
And South they turned below the Po
To halt an army's northbound flow.

Perhaps they may have died in vain
These men who once, beyond this train
Did scarcely note now ancient sites
In desperate prayer sought holy rites.

Of such a loss in blood and treasure
It's hard to gauge the mortal measure
Since few returned to till those fields
Their souls now buried 'neath broken shields

Where once the groves were filled with trees
Of olive fruits well touched by bees
Whose constant flight would scarce abate
Their absent owners' mortal fate.

My heart surveys this ancient route-
The Via Emilia long traced out
From Parma to the Eastern Sea
Coursing through centuries of history.

Jeffry Knuckles
Phippsburg, ME

How a teatro in wood for the third Pope Paul
Became a charter house scene for the author Stendhal,
And a rose-hued fount was reduced to a sight
For cameras of tourists unaware of its might.

After William invaded England's south shore,
Leaving a Tower of stone at London's cold core,
A Duomo in Modena began to arise
Above vineyards and orchards into radiant pale skies.

Today is cloud-filled as our train passes through,
Beyond biblioteca, and a Ferrari or two,
Swept on our way by Pavoratti's aria
An angelicly modern Ave Maria.

Guelphs and Ghibellines near here went to war
As pope and king tallied their score
And generations became but a fuel to the fire,
An inferno of powers with Lombardis for hire.

Peaceful scenes today can barely conceal
Millennia of warfare which seems so surreal
That entering Bologna on a marbled arcade
We nearly forget the price those men paid.

Despite all those years of university courses
Rich students abandoned their books for war horses
In search of vain-glory we can but surmise
Or a less noble territorial expansionist prize.

In Forli we discovered Pinacoteca Domenico
Housing works on the order of Fra Angelico
Not far from the towers around Piazza Cavour
Where a cafe is host to a troubador,

Jeffry Knuckles
Phippsburg, ME

Who sings of a history that preceded this train
Where outside our windows and masked by the rain
Centuries of blood and bone fed the grass
Where armies of tourists now blindly pass.

The Adriatic looms large just up ahead
Where artists and poets are known to have fled
A fascist regime that followed the war
That never quite touched this beautiful shore.

Here Dante in exile by the Guelphs was sent
To Ravenna from Florence for political dissent
Entombed, enshrined, and finally at peace
Rejoined once again with sweet Beatrice.

***

Margaret Roncone
Vashon, WA

Photograph of Snow

Today wind stalks rain
or is it the other way around
when I think of this happening
as the earth tips its axis
I get lightheaded
when I photograph rain
what appears is snow
I'm on a stage with angels
trimming their wings
wind forms green caverns in a cedar
a thousand mouths opening
I listen but all I hear
Is the stage floor creaking.

Juliana L'Heureux
Topsham, ME

Above the Fold

A startling World War II history lesson leaped out of a 1940 newspaper, yellowing with age, in an above the fold headline. It was an obituary tribute calling attention to the high-esteem the deceased nun held among the readers. Finding the 1940 obituary of Ida Lévêque also known as "Sister Myriam," printed in headline font on *Le Messager*, the Lewiston, Maine, French language newspaper, was like visualizing a ghost's image on paper. Reading the news about her life and untimely death during World War II, in France, was reminiscent of experiencing a specter in a dream. She sincerely wanted to be noticed. She was an unlikely victim of the war in France. In fact, the news about her death transcends time, because the sadness described in the circumstances that killed her are universally understood. She was a refugee.

Sister Myriam was killed in a Nazi bomb attack in Northern France during the 1940 fighting in "The Battle of France" (May 10–June 6, 1940). Tragically, along with six other religious sisters, Sister Myriam was killed while the group was trying to escape an attack by the Nazi Luftwaffe. Her death in France was as sad to read in the 21st century, as it must've been to those at the time. An original copy of *Le Messager,* with the news and her above the fold obituary, was donated to the Franco-American Collection at the University of Maine Lewiston Auburn College. Her picture printed in the newspaper was a beautiful portrait of a gracious young lady; evidently, taken before she entered religious life.

Virtually all of the front page news in the 1940 newspaper described the terror of Nazi operations in Europe. But, the lead headline above the fold read, "Une Jeune Relig'euse de Lewiston tuée France." Reading about Sister Myriam's short life created a surprisingly teachable moment, as

Juliana L'Heureux
Topsham, ME

though her spirit somehow touched a pause button in my archival research to find information about Franco-American veterans. Her story was personal evidence about the horror of trying to survive in the midst of a war and the human toll consumed by the carnage. By reading about Sister Myriam's attempt to escape the dangerous escalating war in Europe, we can imagine how her panic continues to be experienced by millions of refugees in modern times.

She was killed by a Nazi bomb. News media in the 21st century hardly ever use the word "Nazi" anymore. In fact, the word is more like an ideological stereotype than a description of the perpetrators of the deadly 1940 Luftwaffe attack. Yet, in the yellow newsprint, every story reported on the front page was about the Nazi invasion of Europe. Although Sister Myriam died in June of 1940 (and the exact date could even have been May 30th), it was not until August that her death was reported. She was described as being a refugee who was fleeing the Nazi "horde." Her family was well known in the Lewiston community because she was the daughter of Maine State Representative and Mrs. Pierre Lévêque of Blake Street. In the Nazi attack, she was killed by a bomb near Béthune, in Northern France. Her family was notified in a letter written by Siser Maria Donimique. "Myriam attempted to flee Béthune in the company of Sister Marie De Bethlehem. When the bombardment began, the sisters took refuge in a small house at the side of the road. Ten other persons were also huddled in the wooden structure when the bomb struck. Seven of them were killed, while the others were severely injured. Sister Marie De Bethlehem was buried in the debris for 19 hours before a group of nuns were able to reach her." But, Sister Myriam did not survive.

Sister Myriam's short life was framed by war. In fact, she was born in Lewiston on August 3, 1914, on the day when the first World War was declared in Europe. At the time, it was supposed to be "La guerre pour mettre fin à toutes les guerres," (The War to End All Wars), but instead, "le der des

Juliana L'Heureux
Topsham, ME

ders" (the end of the end) was the prelude to World War II.

As though it were somehow predestined at the time of her birth, at the onset of World War I, Sister Myriam's life ended in a war. Undoubtedly, in a time when the entire world was consumed by war—and during The Great Depression of the 1930s—Sister Myriam made a choice to dedicate her life to teaching and helping others. Her formal religious life began when she entered the Dominican Order in 1933, in Valleyfield, Quebec. Later, during her stay in France (where the Dominican priests, nuns and brothers have an international headquarters) she was sent to complete her religious studies at the Sorbonne, in Paris. She was scheduled to return home to Lewiston in the fall of 1940 to teach.

It was the pacifist Mahatma Ghandi who inspired the world during those troubled times, when he challenged us to become the change we want to see in the world. Sister Myriam lived the change she hoped to see in the world. Sadly, in her unexpected death in a Luftwaffe attack, the opportunity to inspire others through teaching was ended in Béthune. Yet, in the above the fold obituary, her spirit reached out to teach us today. We can be the change to help the refugees we read about and see on the news today. Sister Myriam created an awareness, in my mind, about how we can strive to be our own "above the fold" news by working for peace and the protection of desperate people who are victimized by wars.

Goose River Anthology, 2017

Elmae Passineau
Weston, WI

Behind the Furnace

The basement had a long narrow room
   where clothes hung and dried
   in the wintertime
It had a wash room
   with a round white washer
   topped with wringers
   next to two deep rinsing tubs
After the clothes chugged around in hot water
   made soapy by dissolved slivers of Fels Naphta,
   Mom taught me how to arrange
   the soaking wet items
   so they would glide smoothly
   through the wringers for the first rinse
   followed by a second trip
   into the bluing water
One more round through the wringers
   and they were ready for hanging
I liked the smell of the soap
   and the humid warmth of the chilly cellar
There was a canning room
   shelves lined with Mom's canned peaches,
   blackberries, pickles, beets....
There was a furnace room
   the old coal furnace as big around as a merry-go-round
   wide arms spoking up to the ceiling
A coal chute funneled chunks of coal
   onto a dusty heap
And behind the furnace room
   was where the ghost lived
I could, if I dared,
   squeeze through a narrow passageway

                                        (continued)

Elmae Passineau
Weston, WI

behind the furnace
   that led to a dim empty room
   strung generously with cobwebs
I did that, a time or two,
   before I decided that facing a ghost
   required more moxie than I had

***

Snow Sweets

Snow day, I whisper
   His tousled hair
   copper against the white pillow
   barely stirs

Snow day, I whisper
   One eye slits open
   still filled with sleep
   and a dream's journey

Snow day, I whisper
   Both eyes spring open, close—
   a slow drowsy grin
   as he squirms with pleasure
   and huddles deeply into the warmth

Later there is a snowman, maybe a snow fort
   and chocolate chip cookies
   we always bake on snow days

Christopher Fahy
Thomaston, ME

Gone

The lawn unruly, tangled,
well on its way to becoming a field,
a hole in the floor of the porch
near the door, which isn't locked,
so we enter the kitchen
and see a long stain
on the wallpaper's flowers
a table, two chairs and a walker
left in the final hour.

The drawer beside the porcelain sink
is open wide and shows us remedies
for high blood pressure, diabetes
rheumatoid arthritis, other tragedies
that carry us away.
The heart pills will expire in three days.

***

Sylvia Little-Sweat
Wingate, NC

Prism

When love was incandescent
hearts blazed red and orange
and glowed with saffron joy.
But then a jade aubade turned
her heart's hue a deeper blue
than indigo. It took a brighter
heart to spark a riot of violet.

Robert B. Moreland
Pleasant Prairie, WI

Impact

Professor stands, a warrior against disease having fought a long campaign begun three decades before. Enemy, a virus of unknown etiology; suspected but long eluded his attempts, his analysis. Then captured at last, dissected and probed, he unlocked its code and secrets until it yielded knowledge to staunch the disease's morbidity. An invited talk in Melbourne, he leaves his work, goes to share. First class seat, settles in reviewing slides and notes, collecting his thoughts. A twelve-hour flight, he has much to do: plans the next steps of future research, protégés to train, grants to write; money to fund the work of a real cure. He smiles, God forbid maybe even a Nobel speech to ponder. Reverie bumped by turbulence, he gazes out the window, lush farmland below. A flash catches his eye. Mesmerized, he sees a wispy tendril reaching upwards to him, a sign from below, beckoning. Blinding flash, his life abruptly ends, molecules of memory dispersed for the six-mile plummet still bound by gravity.[1]

[1] Professor Joep Lange—Department of Medicine, University of Amsterdam—was one of 298 victims of the Malaysian Airline Flight 17 shot down near Hrabove, Ukraine, July 17, 2014.

Richard Taylor
Bethel, ME

East of the Divide
Spring, Browning, Montana

Houses of wood and square, sheds close by, lank barns
shrink to a spare earth at the river's slow bend.

Wind careens through town, barn boards
bang, gutters rattle, gates slap at their latches.

You can get killed by a flying rock, or trip
on a hard spot in the wind, says a man.

A crow falls across the pale sky, mark of lost memory,
the hush of April, the mountain rushing down.

A Blackfeet girl, trim cut black as a wing, knows
no hurry, marble dark eyes gliding along the gravel street

to her school, lifted in the ruffles of her white skirt.
Her step calms the restless stones and three horses

nibbling thin grass among the churchyard graves
beside her playground with a seesaw.

Dust chases their prints away, and hers
have no need to stay. Her fleet smile turns the air,

murmurs soft song from place to place as breath pleases,
easy as wind from the mountain and April.

She is not late, she is not early.

Miriam Nesset
Georgetown, ME

Altruism Is Dead

Beau Michaels entered the work force with the arrogance typical of a twenty three year old with a graduate degree. Environmental issues were his calling. Though he wanted to work for the state, he was determined not to become just another bureaucrat. He would change the world—and he'd start with litter.

After searching all spring and summer, he landed a job with a state environmental agency. As luck would have it, he'd be able to work at home most of the time, checking into the regional office a couple of times a week, to the capital once a month. It was a lovely fall day in late October when he moved to a small town, renting a house in the country on a dead end road near a small, picturesque lake. The countryside was beautiful, with rolling hills, woods, a stream, and fencerows along winding roads. By the time he'd settled into his new home an early snow had fallen, covering the ground. Despite the snow, on milder days, between sessions at the computer, he sandwiched in a walk to the end of his road, where it met the highway—approximately four miles round trip. Occasionally, someone passed him in a car but otherwise he had the road to himself and never met anyone walking. Along the way he'd stop to talk to the cows and horses in his neighbor's field, breathing in the fresh country air (including the smell of manure), and was glad to be away from the hustle of a city.

Coffee cup in hand, he watched the sun rise over the rim of the hill beyond the lake each morning. Deer, opossums, squirrels, and raccoons came frequently to visit. It was a harsh winter. As it grew colder, he went for walks less frequently, instead admiring the world around him from large windows that overlooked the lake. Referring to The Sibley Guide to Birds he identified fifty-seven different species of

Miriam Nesset
Georgetown, ME

birds, including migrating swans and Sandhill cranes.

When spring finally arrived, he started walking again, enjoying the bucolic scenery. Wild flowers began to spring up, the grass turned green, pink and white blossoms filled the windfall apple trees. He picked wild asparagus along the fencerows, eating it like candy, while noting the bounty of wild blackberry bushes from which he could pick when summer arrived. Everything seemed idyll—except for one thing. Never had he seen so much litter. Beer and soda cans and bottles, as well as various other trash, littered the ditches along the roadside. *This is a dead end road*, he said to himself. *Do the people who live here litter their own road and, if so, why would they do that?*

A conservationist in every respect, he was offended by seeing the beautiful countryside littered, and decided something needed to be done about it. Graduate school had taught him nothing if not how to do research—rigorous research, using quantitative data. Though not an explicit hypothesis, he suspected an inverse relationship between the amount of litter and the intelligence of the litterer. Step one would be to come up with a research design that would allow him to arrive at defensible, qualitative conclusions. He'd need to collect the trash, arrange it in categories for analysis, identify the variables then tally the results. If all went well, the study would allow him, in the end, to identify the culprit or culprits, or at least arrive at a general description of the litterer or litterers. Questions swirled: *Were most litterbugs beer drinkers, as appeared evident during a cursory examination of the ditches? If so, what type of beer did they consume before tossing the empty container, glass or can, into ditches or along fencerows?*

There was no doubt that society was fraught with self-indulgence. Here, however, in his research, he was determined to focus on the problem of litter, i.e. the tons of litter along streets, roads, and highways—and specifically on his road. You'd think that by now we'd have heard enough about

**Miriam Nesset
Georgetown, ME**

litter, he mused. Apparently not since the ditches continue to be strewn with it. The only improvement he could see was that it was now picked up and bagged, usually by a state highway department or prisoners, at taxpayer's expense. He was firm in his conviction that those who littered cared nothing for the common good, had no compunction about marring the shared scenic landscape or environment, and were oblivious to or didn't care about the cost of picking it all up. *Picking up after oneself is, or should be, a basic tenet taught by all parents to their young children*, he thought.

To begin any research project, basic assumptions had to be advanced. It was a known fact that 100 was the average IQ of humans. That meant that half of the population had IQs higher than 100, half lower. In line with his inverse relationship theory, once the litter was analyzed, he could assign the highest IQ to consumers who discarded the least number of beverage containers, the lowest IQ to consumers who discarded the most. Anyone who littered logically had to be below the average in intelligence. Therefore, the highest IQ score (least amount of litter) a litterer could receive was 99. The scores would then continue in descending order, with the lowest assigned to those who littered most. Delimitations of the study were that articles of clothing, condom wrappers, cigarette butts, and other stray items of litter which might identify the litterer would not be analyzed, however an analysis of empty cigarette packs would be attempted.

Using his two-mile stretch of dead end road as his study area, he began his research. On daily walks he picked up trash in the ditches, dragging it home to sort and tally in order to compile his data. It took him all summer and most of the fall. He then ranked IQs from highest (for a litterer) to lowest, along with the calculations lowest to highest of the drink of choice for those who discarded their empty containers by throwing, tossing or otherwise ejecting them from the windows of their vehicles. Please note this was not an IQ ranking of the consumers of the beverages listed, only the lit-

Miriam Nesset
Georgetown, ME

terbugs using the road to his house.

IQ of 99: A variety of types of litter but very few items of each. Blatz, Country Time Lemonade, Korbel Brandy, Grape Soda, All Sport, Fruit Punch, A&W Root Beer, Michelob Golden Light, chocolate milk, Coke Classic, Clearly Canadian, Sprite

IQ of 90-94: V-8, Coors Light, Crush, Dr. Pepper, Pabst Blue Ribbon

IQ of 85-89: Pepsi, Miller Genuine Draft, Old Milwaukee, Royal Crown Cola, Ocean Spray Grapefruit Juice

IQ of 80-84: Miller Genuine Draft Light

IQ of 75-79: Diet Pepsi, Old Style

IQ of 70-74: Busch Light

IQ of 65-69: Miller

The numbers then leapt to significantly higher quantities of litter of four types: Busch, Bud Light, Mountain Dew, and Miller Light. This group was combined and assigned an IQ lower than 65.

After all the litter along his two-mile walking route had been picked up and analyzed, he despaired when it began accumulating again. So either the people who lived in the few homes on his road littered their own environment or outside visitors, possibly delivery personnel, were littering. Since there were few deliveries to the homes along the road, he reluctantly concluded that the litterer or litterers lived on his road. To be sure of his conclusions, he redid the study. Over the next several weeks he again gathered litter as it accumulated in the ditches. Thank goodness there was a late snow

Miriam Nesset
Georgetown, ME

so he could complete his analysis. The quantities were smaller, but the results were the same. Though he wasn't definitively able to identify the exact perpetrators, he was able to draw some interesting conclusions as to their behavior and choices.

Those who drank Pepsi rather than Coke were twice as likely to litter.

Some idiot or idiots that lived in or frequented the neighborhood were trashing their immediate environment. Even pigs did not sleep in their own waste.

The alcoholic drink of choice for the litterers along his road was Bud Light, though perhaps they bought this brand because it was on sale, not because of low intelligence.

When not consuming alcoholic beverages, their drink of choice was Mountain Dew. He could only conclude that when not seeking a high with alcohol they were stewed up on caffeine.

The perpetrator or perpetrators were probably male since marking their territory was more typical of that sex.

The litterer or litterers preferred chewing Skoal, smoking Marlboro or Camel cigarettes, and used Bic lighters.

Over the next several months he watched his neighbors, as well as those who frequented the convenience store on the highway into town. With his study in mind, he kept an eye out for a male that appeared highly energetic, fringing on hyperactive, displayed signs of low intelligence (hard to tell sometimes), bought Bud Light or only the beer on sale, pur-

Miriam Nesset
Georgetown, ME

chased Mountain Dew only in plastic bottles, chose Skoal tobacco, a Bic lighter to go with the Camel or Marlboro cigarettes, and loaded up on Frito Lay potato chips and Nabisco chocolate chip cookies. If his left sneaker was missing, and his sock, he'd be the culprit.

In the end defeat was reluctantly admitted. Walking along the road, the words of a professor of environmental psychology while in graduate school haunted him. She said that the least effective means for changing people's behavior was education. Sad as it was, he conceded that it must be true. The anti-litter campaigns of the last several decades had not halted the problem—hadn't even seemed to make a dent in it. She espoused that the most effective method for changing behavior was to hit people in their pocket books but he didn't see that the higher cost of beer and cigarettes, the higher taxes levied, and fines for littering had made any difference. The laws against littering appeared to be unenforceable. Unless someone in law enforcement actually saw a person littering, nothing was done, and even then, rarely. Trying to think of a way to halt the trashing of our environment, he briefly subscribed to the idea of analyzing the fingerprints on discarded trash along the ditches then tracking down and fining the culprits.

He continued to pick up the litter of careless, thoughtless people the two years he lived near the lake. Walking the country roads, enjoying the pristine landscape, he wondered if people ever took time from hectic schedules to look at their surroundings, to see the beauty of a soaring hawk, the crystalline shimmer of snow, the spring green buds and colorful blossoms, the profusion of wild flowers and vines, berries on lush bushes ripening under a summer sun. If they truly noticed these things, if they viewed the landscape as beautiful, treated it with respect, and ascribed to the notion that it was for all to enjoy, he liked to think that they'd be less inclined to litter.

Fountain of Youth

I recall the ample echoing shower room
in the basement of the old Y
where my small daughter and I once bathed
with all the other mothers and children
after Mom and Polliwog Swim Time.
Six shower heads topped off thin pipes
at one long tiled wall. We hard-thumbed
knobs of thick white porcelain to start
the subterranean bumping through the pipes
before we stepped into the promising downpour.

As if it was carnival time for amphibians,
we celebrated the noisy rain.
Round full mothers and slippery
baby-skinned polliwogs,
shrieking our babble of echoing voices
in the sibilant spray of a steam calliope.

I recall bosoms and bottoms,
the fleshy abundance of motherhood,
glossy arms, soapy cheeks and chins,
our little ones on the brink
of losing their wiggling tails,
sprouting toes and bulged bellies.
All of us glistening, reverberating
off-pitched notes of delight
in that warm cloudless fountain of time.

Lilli Buck
Bristol, VA

The Lord's Deep Holy Silence

They found him in Gethsemane,
And they led him away.
They took him to the high priest,
And what did Jesus say?
Nothing, but the Lord's deep holy silence.

They took him to Caiaphas
In the middle of the night.
Jesus would not argue,
Or take up for his own rights.
There was nothing,
But the Lord's deep holy silence.

So they took him to Pilate,
To be put on trial.
Pilate interviewed him,
But he made no denial.
There was nothing,
But the Lord's deep holy silence.

So they took him and whipped him
With scourges and scorn.
But did Jesus cry out
As his flesh was cruelly torn?
No, nothing, but the Lord's deep holy silence.

So they took him back to Pilate,
And showed him to the crowd.
Pilate said, the release of one prisoner was allowed.
Pilate said, "Should I give you Barabbas,
And crucify your king?"

(continued)

Lilli Buck
Bristol, VA

Did Jesus plead for his own life?
No, he said not a thing.
No, there was nothing
But the Lord's deep holy silence.

He had to carry his own cross
Up to Golgotha's hill.
And at least three times
In the street he fell.
Did he cry out for mercy,
Did he cry out for help?
No, there was nothing,
But the Lord's deep holy silence.

They nailed him to the cross,
And he hung there for hours.
But he did not cry out to the heavenly powers,
To come and rescue him,
And take him down.
There was nothing,
But the Lord's deep holy silence.

He called down no curse
On those who tortured him.
No, he prayed, "Father, forgive them,"
And then once more again,
There was nothing
But the Lord's deep holy silence.

"My God, my God, why hast thou forsaken me?"
He cried.
Then he said, "It is finished,"
And he bowed his head and died.
Then there was nothing,
But the Lord's deep holy silence.

Lilli Buck
Bristol, VA

"He was oppressed, and he was afflicted,
Yet he opened not his mouth.
Like a lamb that is led to the slaughter,
Or a sheep that before its shearers is dumb,
So he opened not his mouth."

—Isaiah 53

***

Julia Rice
Milwaukee, WI

The Icicle and the Flood

Hanging ominously from the roof,
the icicle threatens the person below
who never thinks of the danger,
never knows when the knife will fall.
Coating the window it hides the blue sky
of the icy day piercingly bright.

Crashing between floes, the flood
grows from the snow. The town below
does not know of the danger
that flows with fierce force,
It sits calmly in the sun
that brightens the bitter cold.

On a mountain the skiers flash downwards
keeping their boards straight,
leaping mounds with courage,
controlling the jump over each bump,
secure in their skill, masters of mountains,
kings of the winter, dominators of danger.

Caroline Janover
Damariscotta, ME

The 151ˢᵗ Psalm

When the phone rings at 7:00 in the morning, my heart pounds. Would it be a nurse reporting the death of my elderly mother or father? This call was, in fact, from a nursing home. It was not concerning my mother or father, however. The call was from the director of the local nursing home asking if I could come sit with Betty-Mae as she lay dying. Trained in the Compassionate Care Program to work with the "actively dying," I told the director that I'd get dressed, eat a bowl of cereal and be right over.

I rang the buzzer at the Ebb Tide Nursing Home. A nurse opened the door and greeted me warmly. She thanked me for coming on such short notice. As the nurse led me to the patient's room, I asked her to tell me a little about Betty-Mae's life. The nurse explained that Betty-Mae was 92 years old. She'd been born and raised in a local Maine fishing village. Her sons were both lobstermen and not very attentive. Her only daughter was mentally retarded. Betty-Mae's husband, also a lobsterman, was a heavy drinker who died in a car crash years ago. The nurse explained that Betty-Mae feared being alone just as much as she feared dying. She thought for sure she'd be going to hell. She struggled to stay awake and alive. When we walked into the darkened room, a radio was playing soft gospel music. A vase of faded pink carnations sat on a plastic doily by the bed. When the nurse introduced me, Betty-Mae's eyes darted around the room. She twisted the white bed sheet with gnarled, bony fingers. The nurse took her hand and rubbed it gently. "Caroline will sit with you and read from the Scriptures," she said reassuringly. Handing me the Bible, the nurse smiled and quickly left the room.

I randomly opened the Bible to page 183 and started reading Deuteronomy, The Fifth Book of Moses. Stumbling

Caroline Janover
Damariscotta, ME

over the names Hazeroth and Dizahab, my voice trailed off as I tried to sound out Arabah and Kadeshbarnea. Betty-Mae moaned and kicked her spindly legs under the sheets. "These words are too confusing," I said to myself turning to page 576 and the 23rd Psalm. "The Lord is my shepherd, I shall not want," I continued in a more confident voice.

Reading this familiar psalm made me think about my father. He'd been an Episcopal priest until he ran away with my mother's best friend and got defrocked. I thought back to Christmas mornings when I was a child. My little brother and sisters and I would sit under the tree waiting and waiting for Dad to come home from church so we could open our Christmas presents. After the divorce, we opened our presents right away. When Dad moved out and no longer walked me to school, I'd hold out my mitten and pretend to hold God's hand instead. Dad said that God would always be there to protect me even when I got old.

Betty-Mae suddenly lifted her head off the pillow. Her white hair was matted to the back of her head. She smelled of urine and baby powder. "I had to do it," she sputtered in a raspy voice. Her head fell back on the pillow. The nurse walked in and took Betty-Mae's blood pressure. "Now you just relax, Darlin'," she said. "No point in getting so agitated." The nurse gave Betty-Mae a dose of pain medication under her tongue and left the room.

"What did you have to do?" I asked taking Betty-Mae's bony fingers in my hand. She looked up at the ceiling. Her mouth opened and closed but no words came out. I picked up the Bible and thumbed through the worn pages. Betty-Mae groaned and twisted the sheet. Unable to find the psalm I needed, I decided to make up my own. "The Lord sayeth, bring all ye sinners unto me for they shall enter the kingdom of heaven and sittith on my right hand. The Lord Almighty protectith and forgivith all his flock, especially the mortal sinners who shall find the glory of everlasting life and eternal forgiveness in the kingdom of heaven." Betty-Mae stopped

Caroline Janover
Damariscotta, ME

groaning. She stopped twisting the bed sheets. Looking at me wistfully she whispered, "Read that psalm again, the one about the sinners." I repeated, as best I could, the 151 Psalm.

When the nurse came back into the room Betty-Mae was resting peacefully, a faint smile on her pencil-thin lips. "I haven't seen Betty-Mae this calm in days. What did you say to her?" she asked.

I put the Bible back on the bedside table. "This is the way you look when you are about to enter the Kingdom of Heaven," I replied.

Betty-Mae died a few hours later, still holding my hand.

***

Peggy Trojan
Brule, WI

English Class

In March
the problem boy
in the back seat
gave, finally,
a correct answer.
The class
in hushed surprise
turned and
clapped their
smiling pride.
The problem boy
in the back seat
nonchalantly
looking out the window,
blushed.

Roselyn Stewart
Brookfield, WI

Thrill of the Wild

Our adventure in the woods
was exhilarating.
My friend Irene had suggested
we take the walk.
Hills, gullies and under-growth
Impeded our progress.
Often our feet were entangled
and we had to break free.
When a buck with a huge rack ran
close beside us we were both amazed.
He was enormous, majestic and
a bit frightening. We just stood
awestruck. He stopped for a moment,
just long enough for us to get a good
look at him and then leaped passed us.
He disappeared into the woods and
we were left alone to marvel at
his beauty.
That evening at the Crossroads
Tavern we shared our experience.
Our fellow diners all nodded and
revealed similar stories. I felt privileged
to have been given this opportunity to be
so close to a deer in the wild. While
I didn't have a camera, this experience
is etched in my memory forever.

Ellen M. Taylor
Appleton, ME

Spirit Animals

This morning, my mother called me to her room
to watch a doe and her fawn who stood on the tree line:
They turned and looked back at us as though they'd felt
our gaze from the bedside tray where morphine
had been measured for the day.

Maybe they're spirit animals, I whispered.

May be, she answered.

My mother, who carried seven children, all blessed
in the same baptism gown of white cotton and lace;
who led grace before dinner and prayed in the first pew
for seven decades, now isn't sure she believes
in heaven.

The day stretched across the bay,
the sun beaming and fading like faith.
The deer stayed still as statues in the apse
of the side yard, as if to say, *we're here:*
we hear. We'll always be near.
And then they scampered away.

Mark Biehl
Hales Corners, WI

August Heat

That day in summer began.

The morning was stillborn.
Quiet as a breath held.
Like day-old cotton candy.

Stingy gray shade,
Unforgiving
As a counterfeit priest,
Condemning seekers of relief
To the embers of August.

Go and sin no more.

Stillness.

A viceroy ventures forth lazily
To seek moisture from limp trumpets.

Leaves,
Otherwise paralyzed
Twitch,
As in a dream
Of a breezy unforbidden kiss.

Only children move.

Summertime is brief
Like castles of sand.

Mark Biehl
Hales Corners, WI

The sun,
Rebellious and uncaring—
"Till now immobile
In a timeless sky
Begins to slide,
Swallowed by the edge of earth.

Stillness.
Black heat

That day in summer rests.

***

Edie Schmoll
Menifee, CA

Silence

They met under the barren treetops,
on a cliff above the churning sea;
a depressing wintry scene—
the leaves long ago fallen.
They gazed at each other sadly,
not yet a word spoken;
then clasped hands tightly and hugged—
but only for one quiet moment.
I could not hear the words—
but grim faces told the story;
a whispered exchange, brief but intense—
then empty, sad expressions.
Suddenly a silence, and they turned
from each other, and slowly walked away.
I stayed for a while, and stared bleakly
at the surly waves.

Taylor Leddin
Frankfort, IL

This Is...
By Anonymous

This is...my last message to you
This is...me starting anew

This is...learning how to make it alone
This is...mending the heart you turned to stone

This is...understanding what were lies
This is...seeing myself out of your eyes

This is...knowing that I'm worth much more
This is...me finally knowing to close the door

This is...the last time you make me cry
        This is...goodbye

            ***

P. C. Moorehead
North Lake, WI

Family

Child,
borne here,
borne there.
We love.

Family,
born.

Kathy McHugh
Ogunquit, ME

Hanging the Clothes

It's another sunny blue sky windy day in April—another perfect day for hanging the clothes. So I'm out here once again on my deck attaching dripping wet pants and shirts to the line with colorful bright clothespins. You may think that I am making extra work for myself, but I actually enjoy it; treasure it; find meaning in it. It's about memory. It's about tradition and heritage, something almost sacred, for it is about honoring a very special person whom I've known for forty years—my French-Canadian, ex-mother-in-law—"Memere." Now eighty years old she feels badly that she can't do all she used to: the daily baking, driving, shopping, washing, folding—tasks which gave her a sense of accomplishment and peace; labors of love rather than work.

While raising her family she often did four to five washings each day, proudly bringing out each in the wicker basket to her umbrella-like clothesline, displaying the white and colored items in the sun, in a sort of competition with her neighbors, one whom greeted her from an upstairs window from a pulley clothesline.

When I met Memere she was forty and still working at the shoe shop in the stitching room, where I would often meet her with a pizza on lunch breaks. I marveled at her making taffy in the snow, making string beans in the pressure cooker, and how she treasured her early Saturday mornings reading all the newspapers of the week, the only time of peace in the house when raising three sons. She also enjoyed having a cigarette out by the pool and listening to country music on the radio. I loved her stories about going out to dances and winning jitterbug contests, going roller skating with friends at a popular local rink while their boyfriends were away in Korea before getting married. She treasured her trips to the Grand Ole Opry and Branson, Missouri as well as Florida

Kathy McHugh
Ogunquit, ME

and her favorite destination—Myrtle Beach. I marveled at her growing up and speaking fluent French with her parents who continued to live upstairs in the same household.

I once went with her to Thetford Mines, Canada where I ended up needing Memere as a translator even though I had studied Parisian French for seven years. I had learned basic expressions and words like table, drink, restaurant, bathroom and egg, but not words I needed to order food like scrambled or fried. One summer she had me wait in the yard for her Canadian relatives to arrive while she went to the store, and when they got there I became nervous and forgot every expression I had ever learned in French. I wanted to ask them how long it took them to get there, but instead we nodded and smiled a lot until she got back.

Memere enjoyed waitressing in the restaurant she and her husband owned, also playing cards, having company, going to class reunions and belonging to a camping chapter. I especially admired her being a devoted person of faith who rarely missed saying the rosary, going to mass and attending Holy Days of Obligation, providing me with prayer books and cards. I followed in her footsteps to a well-known inspiring shrine, a journey I will never forget.

Memere cared about me, and was the age my real mother would have been. She became good friends with my adoptive mother and they often chatted and cheered each other up. She felt badly that as a teen I wasn't allowed to go to dances and parties as she was. Being an only child, her friends became substitute sisters and brothers whom she continued to maintain friendships with for years, many whom have since passed away. There is only one left from her wedding party.

Now that she's older her devoted husband does the wash, cooks the meals, drives the van and keeps track of the numerous doctor appointments and homecare visits. Their jitterbug and travelling times have been replaced by occasional trips to the local donut shop to meet with friends.

Kathy McHugh
Ogunquit, ME

After years of admiring her insightfulness and energy, these days I find myself consoling Memere as she cries in silence during her breathing treatment, claiming she is not good for anything anymore, that she never thought it would come to this, that she doesn't want to interrupt my day. No one hears us but God. I tell her everything will be all right, that I'll always help her. I don't mind at all. I love our visits. I miss the old days too, and all we did as still matters, doesn't fade away even though her sons and mine are now good husbands and fathers in their own communities.

It's almost October and I reach into the container for the clothespins, attaching shirts, pants and towels upside down on the clothesline. The air is cooler at this time of year, but not yet cold enough to turn them into stiff flat boards. I go over to help her put summer clothes away and air out the winter ones: sparkly purple gloves and navy pants, thick pink and gray slipper socks and scarves, green and white gingham nightgown and flannel robe that raise up like spirits waving in brisk wind. I go back in to visit for awhile, later coming back out to unclip the clothespins, draping the cool linens over my shoulder, bringing them inside so she can help me fold them.

Winter was hard. She couldn't go out much, even for church, as the wind was too cold for her breathing. Memere was brought by ambulance from home to hospital to rehab to home, then back to the hospital, and got quite discouraged and confused, but she still trusted me. "You're a true one," she told me on the phone, "and I'll never forget all you've done for me. I know you're thinking of me, praying for me. I think my life is over. I'm not going to get better anyway. I just hope it isn't painful."

As spring approached, she entered the scary world of being tested for dementia, she had headaches and went back to bed after meals and sleepless nights. I checked on her daily, being careful not to call and wake her or her husband up or interrupt home health visits.

Kathy McHugh
Ogunquit, ME

    I'll always think of Memere when I hear a country or 1950's jitterbug song, pass the donut shop or speak a little French with a tourist, but especially on a perfect sunny windy bright blue sky day when I'm out here hanging the clothes…

***

F. Thomas Crowley, Jr
Lincolnville, ME

Spring Medicine

In the spring
I take my medicine
in coffee spoons.

small doses of
new-made maple syrup
overflowing the spoon
into hot coffee.

Healing the
wounds of winter
as the earth warms
and the sun rises
over the islands
sooner every day.

Maine.

Wily Wind

The fickle old wind
has many faces:
It caresses tree
Leaves.
Howls when lifting
shingles on the roof.
On yawls sails billow.
The wind is hot and
dry in the desert.
In woods
wind moves through
pines with a rushing
sound.
When wicked it forms
a funnel cloud.
In winter, stings your face,
freezes your fingers.
Furious hurricanes
wreak havoc.
Yet on warm summer
nights it makes music
as it flutters wind chimes.

Trudy Wells-Meyer
Scottsdale, AZ

A Young Girl Trapped in an Old Body
For Aunt Bessie

Each moment is a place you've never been.
                              –Mark Strand

To live to 99 in the circle of life—moving in and out of
time, a circle of memories;
a mile-stone birthday, the exceptional kind.
At Dakota Sky Manor we celebrate life, Aunt Bessie's
profound regal air, her sense of humor, gigantic love for
laughter; infectious characteristics for us all.

Family from far listening to her chatter as divine
softness comes over her wrinkled face, to let us know
she is speaking of love, stories from her youth spill out
at a slow pace showing her lower missing teeth.
Bessie stops at moments to catch her breath, or,
simply overwhelmed by memories like
random photographs: the stars seen from her tiny room,
dreamy eyes talking of Papa,
his rare almost smile, and Mama, oh, to pretend
to be a child again . . . as Bessie slumps,
in a worn-out chair; home now, in a corner.

Today, magnificent flowers for a rare extraordinary day,
one balloon with that magic number 99,
few get to live and see.
A nurse tries to ignore Bessie, her cry for help, for a
simple act of needing to go. "I can't lift you alone"
Horse shit, Bessie barks,
I begged yesterday . . . you want me to pee in my pants?
Bessie cuddles a bear with pink polka dots, Dolly,
her name for a stuffed toy-bear,
that traveled from Arizona, not to ever be alone.

Trudy Wells-Meyer
Scottsdale, AZ

Aunt Bessie, a strong link in a growing family chain,
Swiss born, me, from far across the sea; some ties are
simply meant to be.
Bessie talks about her long-passed brother, my husband
Luke's Dad, I hope to hear something, anything,
to understand this thoughtful brilliant genius, Bessie's
adored nephew, my love for thirty-eight blissful
romantic years. My changed life forever—I had only
to see Luke once and feel his gentle touch; the end of
the life I knew, because of a kiss, as if now
responsible for the scene in front of me.

Bessie's soon centenarian eyes not able to see, yet her
mind can, she whispers: *I see the way Luke looks at you.*
A quiver in her voice and extreme tilted head: don't go.
A promise, unbreakable by distance, nor time, to
come back and visit, again, anytime soon.
Bessie will know we carry her in our hearts, as she
grasps Dolly to hold tight—when she is alone.

Thank God, her twin daughters, Luke's cousins nearby,
stop daily at the home for the old. A mother's lost son
for far too long, flies from Florida, a trip to the sun,
see his Mom—led by his guilty emotion,
after life's family heartaches . . . a new-found gratitude,
when it matters most.
The fact after days of rain the sun decided to shine
compels one to believe and smile: it's never too late
when God's abundant love, peace and healing . . .
His presence is with you.
The theft of the past, a distant memory.

Goose River Anthology, 2017//187

Trudy Wells-Meyer
Scottsdale, AZ

A simple good-bye kiss seeming like nothing, yet
everything only too soon, I can feel Bessie's tears;
I smile without much joy, though still a smile.
The image of her anguish forces me to close my eyes—
oh, not to ever be left alone.

We feel the vital need to stop one more time, witness
immense joy in her eyes, again, as if every minute
spent doing something else is wasted time.
Those moments repeat in my mind like a song,
impossible to forget, as we fly West, back home;
I marvel, will someone, anybody, someday come and
see us? Will it matter at all at an age when we admit
staring at sunsets longer, humbly knowing contentment
is luxury—a gift—one of God's immeasurable
blessings and remember:
True happiness is, to want what you have.

***

Patrick T. Randolph
Lincoln, NE

In Laughter and Hugs on the Porch

My wife reads to our little daughter
Under a mid-October sky,

Prairie breezes blow, Mountain ash leaves
Dance and then stop

To listen to our daughter ask questions,
And my wife answer with laughter and hugs.

Diana Coleman
Rockland, ME

Road Trip

Driving a loop around the States and part of Canada was a fun, meditative journey.

Taking such a trip on my own was risky I was warned. My car could break down, I could get lost, or meet up with unsavory characters. *Wasn't I worried?* I didn't know where I would stay most of the time and expected to find inexpensive inns along the way with a few planned stops with family and friends. I looked forward to it.

Departing Maine in mid-October on an alternating sunny and rainy day, driving through a double-rainbow, and traversing country roads lined with autumnal splashes of red, orange and gold-leafed trees was a good start.

Signage along the way caught my attention.

In New Hampshire, a sign announced "Falling Rock." *What are you supposed to do about that? Prepare to swerve as a boulder may come tumbling down on top of you?* I ducked while driving past.

Later that first day, I approached Canada in a blinding snow squall and frigid temperatures. After examining my passport, the border patrol woman asked why I chose the Canadian route since Washington state was my westernmost destination. "Because my phone said so," I replied. She laughed and waved me through. Traveling through Canada would enable me to see part of that country I hadn't been to before. The roads were excellent. Aside from the ubiquitous Tim Horton's at the contemporary glass "On Routes," Canada's version of "Service Areas," the convenient food stops were unfortunately the same—McDonalds, Starbucks, KFC, Denny's.

The highway signs of our northern neighbor are clear and attractive—bright blue with large white lettering. There were wheat, corn and cotton fields. Cotton fluffs flew through the air. Numerous Wal-Mart double-trailer trucks cruised along.

Diana Coleman
Rockland, ME

First dinner out at Aunt Lucy's family restaurant in Kingston, Ontario was a lucky find—fish with a glass of Pinot Grigio. Woke up from the bed and breakfast inn to frozen nasturtiums outside the front door and an icy windshield.

It was Canada's campaign season and Justin Trudeau was the prime minister candidate in fall 2015. Political signs decorated side streets. No billboards were posted on the highways, but there were warnings announcing "Injure or Kill a Worker $7,500 and 15 years." Reentering the States near the Michigan border brought pot-holed roads, narrow lanes and blowing trash. In Wisconsin, a sign announced, "Home of the Butterburger." I imagined large grilled butter pats on a bun. A Mousehouse Cheesehaus, its roof adorned with a large mouse eating a cheese wedge, advertised "Best of Wisconsin Cheese." There were miles of dried corn stalk fields. Wisconsin Dells was a picturesque lake resort surrounded by pines, birch and muted fall colors—golds, ambers and rusts.

Minnesota showcased a large billboard of a young boy with a basketball, "Teen Depression." Another sign said: "Helping Farm Families in Crisis" by FarmRescue.org. In Fargo, North Dakota, a trailer truck hurried past carrying a long, articulated San Francisco MUNI bus like one I formerly rode as a resident of that city. *What was it doing in Fargo?* Also saw my first triple trailer Fed Ex truck. Three of them in a row went by. *Were all nine trailers filled with packages?*

Montana, advertising "Treasure State" on its license plates, had spectacular scenery. It was like driving through a postcard. In one sweeping glance there were green grassy fields, cliffs with pine trees, dried corn stalk fields, yellow-leafed Aspens glowing in the sunlight alongside a river, and snowy mountains set off by an azure blue sky. A train with billowing smoke moved snake-like in the distance. There were Angus beef ranches and fields with gigantic steel, spidery legs for spraying and neatly stacked hay balls like straw wine kegs. A sign proclaimed, "Wild Life Crossing Next Mile."

Diana Coleman
Rockland, ME

What and where? I prepared to brake for whatever animal would come leaping out. The Continental Divide, crossing over 6,393 feet, was a slow-going climb on the steep mountain road.

Idaho warned: "Transport of Invasive Species Prohibited" followed by "Game Crossing Next 4 Miles." Again, I was on alert for whatever creatures dared cross in front of me.

For such a beautiful and lush state, Washington's welcome sign was understated. It was a small, barely noticeable, "Welcome to Washington." They must have been short on money when this sign was erected. Likewise, Maine's welcome is no better with its bright blue narrow sign with white lettering: "Maine the Way Life Should Be, Open for Business." It sounds like a plea.

There were many wind turbines in Washington—silver blades spinning on hillsides and in flat fields along with hundreds of solar panels. At the Columbia River Gorge rest stop with its stunning deep blue water, there was only one other car in the parking lot. An older couple also marveled at the view. The woman told me, "My son says, 'Off-season travelers are either newlyweds or half-dead.' I guess we are the half-deads," she said. We laughed though in my sixties, I don't consider myself "half-dead" and don't take my life for granted either.

Drought-stricken California had numerous signs along the highway about farmers and the water crisis. "Build Water Storage Tanks Now," and "Farmers Use Water To Do Something Amazing: Grow Your Food—FarmFacts.org." There were miles of fields with stubble—crops gone by or dried up before maturity? In Kern County, a sign said, "Severe Dust Next 40 Miles." Palm Springs was surrounded by huge wind turbines planted in the sand and hills. Near Coachella, signs warned of wind storms and "Avoid overheating—Turn off air conditioning next 10 miles." There were short green pines and scrub brush. Sand swirled and wind gusts were fierce. Another sign said, "State Prison Next

Diana Coleman
Rockland, ME

Exit—Do Not Pick Up Hitchhikers."
   Arizona's large border sign "The Grand Canyon State Welcomes You" was bright yellow. A rest area sign told tourists, "Poisonous snakes—Stay on the path." *Do reptiles know to stay off the path?* There were recreational vehicle sales lots, casino signs, gaming resorts. Tall and stately saguaro cactus rose up in the sand among dark and light colored rocks. A lonely dollar store sat in the small, rundown town of "Salome Where She Danced." Curious about this dancing woman, I read that the town was named after a 1945 war film of the same title, featuring a dancer who traveled from Vienna to this remote outpost which was robbed by bandits as she attempted to make her dancing debut. She then moved West.
   "Hope"—with a tiny church—was another depressing town which announced after a couple of blocks, "Your [sic] Leaving Hope." Derelict gas stations stood with broken windows and grass tufts sprouted through asphalt. Sitting near a defunct gas pump, a large man had his head down—a whiskey bottle by his side. There were RV parks and not much else. Crosses festooned with plastic flowers perched by the side of the road proved there had been car deaths here. Prescott Valley emerged with curvy roads and prominent "Guns and Ammo" signs, beige rocks, and yellow-leafed trees. Traveling west through Arizona, sand blew over vast areas; tumbleweeds flew across the highway.
   After stopping for breakfast at a lonesome café and pulling out sharp needled tumbleweeds from under my car's bumper, I was cautioned by a waitress that there were 65 mph wind gusts along the highway and to stay away from trailer trucks. Dodging tumbleweeds for miles, they were giant balls of straw bouncing along the flat, empty roads except for the occasional trailer truck.
   White and rust striped cliffs emerged with New Mexico's "Land of Enchantment" welcome. There were more "High Wind" signs. Gallup proclaimed, "Most Patriotic Small Town

Diana Coleman
Rockland, ME

in America." *What gave it this distinction?* It was a plain town with a pawn shop and an adult bookstore. Red cliffs appeared with low, dark green trees. A double-car freight train traveled parallel to the road. A sign said, "Elk Next 7 Miles" and billboards publicized, "Whole Lot of Kicking Casino Hotel," and "World Famous Laguna ½ Lb. Burger." There were more casinos. The Indian Pueblo Cultural Center had discount cigarettes. Around Albuquerque, multiple billboards advertised "Fireworks" and Lisa's Truck Stop announced a shooting range. Another sign stated "Prescription painkillers can be as deadly as heroin." A humongous American flag billboard said, "We Believe in America. Public Welcome."

Straw grass plains stretched for miles. Scattered truck tire carcasses lay in huge pieces along the roads. These black twisted shards looked like contemporary sculpture. Near Adrian, Texas, there were thousands of enormous wind turbines. Billboards stated: "Top of Texas Catholic Superstore" and "Got Weed? Call if you got busted." There were novelty fantasy superstores and miles of black and white cows behind metal fences. Cadillac Ranch's car fenders protruded from dirt. Boasting "Big Texas Steak," a billboard pictured a huge steak. The Silver Creek Casino sign advertised "Leave the underwear. We provide the luck."

In Memphis, I devoured a scrumptious salad with beef tips at Marlowe's Restaurant surrounded by Elvis Presley memorabilia and his soulful voice from the jukebox. Touring Elvis's opulent Graceland mansion was fascinating—including his glittery awards and flashy outfits.

After coasting through "Sweet Home Alabama," dinner beckoned near Atlanta. A crowded Cracker Barrel was a new experience with its white meal of chicken and dumplings and grits topped with shredded white cheese. Thick and starchy, the tasteless food stuck together. North Carolina's welcome sign announced "Nation's Most Military Friendly State." At a large, packed barbecue café, I had the 55+ senior plate

Diana Coleman
Rockland, ME

luncheon special—barbecued pork, hush puppies, collard greens and green beans with vinegar—a heavy but delicious meal.

Religious signs à la "It Is Okay to say I love God and to Pray," gospel churches and pawn shops galore lined the roads. Entering Southern Pines, the maples were turning red and tall stands of long needled pine trees stood whispering as the wind passed by. Bone chilling weather hit approaching Maryland. In Manhattan, I found street parking by my East Village hotel for three days. Driving New York City's congested streets surrounded by speedy cabs contrasted with the West's open highways. After stopping in Massachusetts for a family Thanksgiving, it was back to boldly cold Maine.

8,313 miles and 51 days later, Ruby, my red Toyota Rav-4, returned me home. I saw many people along the way—none proved disagreeable. Avoiding massive tumbleweeds and keeping Ruby on the road in gale force headwinds were the biggest challenges. Ruby was thoroughly checked out before departing and re-checked and her oil changed on the West Coast. All was fine.

***

Patrick T. Randolph
Lincoln, NE

Without You

The first Thanksgiving
Without my father—it's been
Four months since his death;

Feel a hand on my shoulder,
Hear his voice—and I give thanks.

Art Schmitz
Milwaukee, WI

A Periodical Question

The erudite environment was enveloped
With the pursuit of periodical investigation
The constant sober mien of the human dignity
Performing her vital duties of serious consequence
Recording, lending, questioning, directing
And returning transactions of periodical literature
For a single cataclysmic moment of beauty rare
Revealed an inner transcendental joy
In serving all
As with August respect for mankind's urgent quest for
    knowledge
She directed the little boy to the restroom
At the end of the adjacent hall

* * **

Mark Biehl
Hales Corners, WI

Song Spirit

Disguised in elegant black
With epaulets of
Red and gold
Faithful ebony angel
Keep me in your watch.

My friend

My love

Sing on.

Donna Bruno
Ft. Lauderdale, FL

English Class

I stand before my teenage students
    Speaking of Homer's "Odyssey"
Of Penelope, Ulysses' faithful and long-suffering wife
    Who waited twenty years for reunion with her husband.
Before me sit kids who fall in and out of love each week.

I laud "The Bard"
    Shakespeare and his masterpieces
The boys see only the curvacious "masterpiece"
    Of the svelte but buxom female blond
Who floats across the room.

I speak of poets
    Byron, Shelley, Keats
"A thing of beauty is a joy forever."
    They nod approvingly
As the same female student
      Demonstrates "poetry in motion" in her walk.

Remember John Donne
    who wrote "No man is an island unto himself."
And with that quote, they recall the hijinks
    Of last week's boozy island beach party
With bombed-out babes.

Do I "cast pearls before swine?" I wonder
    The bell rings—class ends
A student approaches and requests that I peruse his poems;
    I take them home; that night I read them.

Donna Bruno
Ft. Lauderdale, FL

Can it be that this sleepy-eyed, tattooed boy
    Has actually "heard" me?
He writes of "A thing of beauty"
    The Statue of Liberty that welcomed him from a
        distant land.
Ruled by some "MacBeth-like" tyrant—ruthless and
    ambitious.

And identified with "No man is an island"
    When a church group sheltered his family
And led him to this place
    Where in due time, he plans to "march to his own
        drummer."

And so my teacher's "heart leaps up
    when I behold" not Wordsworth's "rainbow in the sky"
But rather one student
    With whom these works have resonated
Words that will be woven
    Into the "masterpiece" tapestry of a life.

                ***

Sylvia Little-Sweat
Wingate, NC

Dirge

Amid seedpods and cockleburs
the frost weeds wait sentient,
white, in the dark of summer's
sarcophagi. Morning glory vines
wind stalks dry as fodder. Curled,
brittle blades of corn, splintered
by wind, rasp winter's warning.

Manny Fiori
San Francisco, CA

Brooklyn Ghost

She walks
Carefully
Tip toeing
The ledge
She receives verbs
Through osmosis
Read right
To left
A bullet
With verve
Moonskin, she is
Sunbone
Epicurean dancer
Teeters
On the edge
Asking of gargoyles where
Latin musicians roam
Looking for
Merengue and mambo players
Up in the Bronx
Once invisible
No more.

Stephen Bloom
Falmouth, ME

Frames of Reference

He opened the door to his apartment, tired and relieved to be back, his arms loaded with three weeks of accumulated mail. He dropped the mail on his desk and his duffel bag on the sofa, then turned on the radio to hear that the fragile ceasefire in the Middle East had broken down in a new wave of suicide bombings. "Damn!" he uttered to himself, although news of the resumption of violence held no surprise—only sadness. His cameras, still unpacked, carried fresh images of the horrific results of human hatreds in that desperate part of the world. The pictures were exceptionally good, he knew, but they would make no difference. That hadn't concerned him much when he was younger. Now, he admitted to himself, it had begun to.

He put water on for tea, then sorted through his mail. It was mostly bills and circulars, and he tossed them on his desk. He set aside a check from some free-lance work, then paused when he noticed a small blue envelope. It was postmarked two weeks ago, the handwriting on it still familiar. He thumbed it open.

"Your father passed away last week," he read. "I thought you should know. He was cremated. There was a small memorial gathering at Union Hall on the 20th. Burial will be some time next spring. I'll let you know, if you want. Love, Ellen."

That was all his sister had written. No betrayal of sadness or regret on her part; no expectation of remorse or anything else from him. Not even a copy of a newspaper obituary, although he was sure there would have been one in *The Labor Guardian*, the newsletter his father had written for and edited for more than 20 years.

Her note was folded inside a blank greeting card. The drawing on the front was of a single, slightly drooping fox-

Stephen Bloom
Falmouth, ME

glove, growing amid weeds alongside the stone foundation of a neglected old farmhouse. He wondered briefly if his sister had meant a subtle insult by that flower, known for both its healing and poisonous qualities. No, he thought. More likely she only meant the image to represent the sadness of a useful life ended, the loneliness of death, and the comfort of memory. Ironically, it was a sentiment that would have been humbug to his father. For himself, he took no offense either at the image or at the tardiness of the notice. His estrangement from both of them was long established.

Older by a year, Ellen had stayed at home, alone with their father for all that time. He was never sure if her devotion was simply to him or to his political causes as well, which in any case she had helped him to promulgate. *It wouldn't matter*, he told himself. If you take the man, you take his obsessions.

Out of courtesy, at least, he made room for the card and propped it open on the file cabinet beside his desk.

His was a small apartment on the backside of Sutton Place in New York City. He occupied it only occasionally now that he was away so often on assignment. It was in an old, well-maintained six-story building with elevator and security. He had chosen it years ago because its size had made it affordable. Now that he could afford more he had little interest in moving, even though his constant absence was beginning to make him feel like a stranger in these rooms. Still, the place continued to give him easy access to airports, protection for his expensive equipment, and a peaceful sanctuary.

Besides some essential pieces of furniture, the apartment was sparse. A few paintings and prints by artists he knew had been framed and hung stylishly by Carla, a former lover who had hoped to live among them. Most of the other surfaces were given over to his own images—mostly in black and white, the medium he had made his own. There were proofs and experimental layouts and a few award winners and dry-

Stephen Bloom
Falmouth, ME

mounted favorites that depicted the range of his interests and assignments: the details of nature and commerce, architecture and people—and war.

He turned his gaze out the window at the small panorama of the neighborhood below: the human activity on the street, the little private park across the avenue just off the corner. Again he admired the gentle unity of the older architecture and the inconsonant but somehow harmonious street-level commerce in this part of the city.

Ordinarily, the view from the window drew him compulsively to a project he had begun shortly after he had rented the apartment. Years before he had been moved by an exhibit of the work of Pissarro, the Impressionist painter who, confined to his Paris apartment by poor eyesight, produced not quite identical cityscapes from his window, each enclosed in distinctly different frames of reference—wonderful images by themselves, stunning and provocative seen together. Inspired, he had begun aiming his cameras out the window, trying to isolate pedestrians within the busy life on the street, always using the same vantage but without any of the new digital artifices of his craft. Instead, he used a variety of lenses, and relied simply on composition, focal length, available light, and timing. As with most of his work, he used only black and white film, producing harsh images that viewers needed to study to be rewarded. He thought that at some point he might mount a solo exhibition or produce a book, if the complete pictorial effect promised to say anything new about the reality of modern life. He had sought Carla's opinion of the photographs. She had been critical, even disturbed.

"You cut all your people off from each other. They seem to be floating down there without any purpose. That's not the way they are, not the way they look to me, even from up here. You make them all so lonely."

She might just as well have added: "Just like you."

Stephen Bloom
Falmouth, ME

He had picked the wrong time to ask. Her response seemed to unfold out of the most recent of their increasingly frequent arguments about their future.

"That's not really fair," he had defended. "Photographically, those people are just objects. I'm only looking for ways to emphasize the visible connection between individuals and their physical environment—their places on the sidewalk, or the street, or the doorways where they shop or live. I don't really care where they've been, or where they're going, or what they're thinking. They're just figures—there, at that moment. I'm not trying to manufacture some imaginary emotions you may think they ought to have."

He had regretted his tone even more than his choice of words. It was true that he had invited her comments, but her observations had forced him to defend his pictures too soon, before he had actually worked out a coherent meaning for the project. He knew he needed to think more deeply about it before he could consider showing or publishing the images. Yet he suspected that what he had said would turn out to be fairly accurate, regardless of how spontaneously defensive his reaction to her criticism had been.

Neither Carla nor his father had understood his objectivity—his urge to witness widely without active involvement with his subjects, involvement that he was sure would narrow his view. He wanted to stay separate from others, and to see and record as much as possible without political alignment or cause.

His father had been active in the labor movement, and had lost his job as a steamfitter in an unorganized factory because of his sympathies. He then began to write for a small, radical labor newsletter, which broadened his anger. His writing became more theoretically socialist, and by the time he eventually assumed editorial control of the newsletter, the incompatibility of labor and management had become an obsession—one that ruled the rest of his life.

Stephen Bloom
Falmouth, ME

At the last, his father had been too busy to attend his high school graduation. Afterward, he had yelled at his father, arguing that his single-minded partisanship made it impossible for his father to see the world with any nuance, with anything other than predetermined biases. It was an addiction, undermining the value of everything else, rendering life colorless, leaving no free choices; not even the ability to be disillusioned with the movement he championed.

"Unlike you," he had screamed, *"I still have choices."*

And he had left.

His sister, despondent, heard it all but didn't, or couldn't, intervene. Ellen had had her own fights with their mother who, she thought, didn't put any effort into understanding their father. He remembered his sister as a lonely, intelligent girl, dependable and pragmatic where their father was meteoric and ideological. Throughout their high school years, she had defended their father against her mother's frustration, and those fights seemed to solder her loyalty to her father. Their mother had finally walked away, leaving a belligerent but helpless man in the charge of his two teenaged children. He knew, and regretted, that his departure soon afterwards had probably consigned his sister to her life of loyal servitude.

Across the hall a door slammed, wrenching him with a cringe from one memory to another.

Far away a bomb would be exploding. The crowd in the marketplace would scatter. In the fierce, searing silence immediately following the concussion, survivors close to the blast would have an eerie, slow-motion awareness of isolated details—black smoke, then fire, then fragments of glass, stone, and bricks, then blood and bloodied things, all slowly accumulating, taking form like exposed photo paper in the darkroom developer bath.

Eventually, people would emerge from behind dusted parked or ruined vehicles, from doorways, from behind the corners of buildings and side streets, and from the shelter of

Stephen Bloom
Falmouth, ME

rubble from their disintegrating city. Amid the soft, shimmering sound of fire, and the sluggish crescendo of cries, whistles, and distant sirens, people would move toward some form of safety or purpose. Some would run towards safer refuge, some towards the blast site. Some would stay where they were, too shocked to respond. Others would turn to their technology—their cell phones or cameras, creating history.

Finally, he identified his own cell phone ringing.

"*Welcome back. Settled in, yet? Listen . . ,*" said his editor, not waiting for an answer.

"*Got another assignment for you. Guess you probably heard—ceasefire didn't hold. So. There's an anti-Israeli demonstration Saturday. Down in D.C. Looks to be a fairly big one. We'll need photos. You know, crowd shots, signs, close-ups, speakers and protesters, police, arrests, side demonstrations, etc. Stuff you're best at.*"

Complete sentences always suffered as much as solicitude when his editor needed to persuade.

"Oh, c'mon, Stanley, I can't. I just . . ." he started to protest. But his editor rushed on:

"*Help you decompress. You've just seen the conflict over there first-hand. You'll get better stuff than Carter ever could. Sending Joe Douglas along to write the story. Coordinate with him. You've got his number. In the West Village.*"

"Good. So," he continued, "*I assume you've got something from the trip? Get what you have over to me today, and we'll work on it here. This'll give you a couple of days to relax, talk to Joe and get down to D.C. When you get back we'll still have another couple of days before deadline to go over layout.*"

He argued, finally accepted, then closed his phone and leaned against the window frame. He looked out again, searching absently for a pedestrian to photograph. Mostly he saw the noisy, one-way yellow traffic rushing silently uptown. Pedestrians on the avenue looked frenetic and single-minded, obscuring any detail of interest. His eyes were

Stephen Bloom
                                             Falmouth, ME

diverted instead to the little gated park on the side street across 1st Av.

The gate was open. A woman—he wondered if she was a mother or perhaps a nanny?—sat calmly on one of the green wrought-iron benches talking with a small white-haired woman who was knitting something in a splash of red yarn. Nearby, a small group of young children tussled in the grass with a big, happy dog. The scene was tranquil, comforting. He wondered what they were saying to each other.

He eased himself down in his desk chair, closed his eyes, and leaned his head back. For the only time he could remember, he found himself wondering what his father would think of the pictures he had brought back.

After a moment, he turned away from the window, re-opened his phone, dialed information, and asked for the number for his sister.

                          ***

                                          Patrick T. Randolph
                                          Lincoln, NE

Complex Simplicity of a Sigh

Unique moment on a city bus,
I hear an elderly homeless man sigh,

And in the brief song of his breath,
I can hear the chorus of his life—

A musical performance beyond anything
Broadway could even hope to produce.

Sylvia Little-Sweat
Wingate, NC

Going Home

Going home, going home I'm just going home.
Quiet like some still day I'm just going home.

On the porch of Faulks Baptist Church this May morning—a table spread with personal memories of a Union County farm, a few shucked whole ears of harvested corn, jars of gold seed-corn, and a plaque honoring one who measured many fields before—all mute eulogies to a life of farming.

I'll Fly Away
Some bright morning when this life is o'er,
I'll fly away to that home on God's celestial shore.

Joel Rufus Smith, ninety-five when he died Sunday morning, left all life behind for a grave next to one, long with grass overgrown. He left his three sons, nine grandchildren, and twelve great grandchildren, tilled wheat and corn fields, and a large garden that he plowed, planted, hoed, and picked last summer.

What A Day That Will Be
When He takes me by the hand and leads me through
the promised land, what a day, glorious day that will be.

Bernice Webb Smith has been waiting thirty-four years for her husband to come to the heavenly home. Sisters and brothers have been waiting more recently. Spring fields and boundaries of distant trees encircle the tranquil church cemetery on a rising hill. Today it is filled with sunshine, birdsong, gentle breeze.

Sylvia Little-Sweat
Wingate, NC

Amazing Grace

*'Tis grace hath bro't me safe thus far,
And grace will lead me home.*

A service that began as the old church bell was rung
ends when all the verses of *Amazing Grace* are sung.
Graveside rites now done, family free snow-white doves—
three to be the Trinity and one to be a Soul, now alone,
ascending infinity, seeking by grace to join the Trinity.
At last Joel Rufus Smith is going home, just going home.

***

Sharon Lask Munson
Eugene, OR

Java Tattoo

The young waitress' bright bouquet
blooms out of her ample bosom,
spills across slim shoulders
down to the hand holding the pencil
taking my latte order,
taking my breath.

Lipstick red roses
pucker up to blue delphinium
while masses of zinnias, hollyhock and phlox
play peek-a-boo
under her scooped neck
short-sleeved, white cotton tee.

A sweep of colors captivates;
she pours coffee, makes change.

Jean Lawrence
Waldoboro, ME

Stately Mansion

Stately mansion on a hill
built to display to all
the due reward of power and position,
you were your designer's showplace,
the symbol of his creed: "the right of the good, the wise,
    and the rich to govern."
Like your creator, you rose in status and value as the years
    rolled by.
However, you outlived your original master
and grew to national prominence for your historical value.
For two hundred years, admiration and homage were yours.
People viewed you with awe and dreamed of days long gone.
Few knew anything about the man who built your walls
and etched his name pridefully on your foundation.
Your fame came from your beauty and age.
But, beauty can fade and age decays.
Even monuments to wealth and position fall.

'Inspired by the destruction by fire of the Reed Mansion,
April 2, 2017

***

Sylvia Little-Sweat
Wingate, NC

Pansies

Parading motley—
harlequin faces sunward—
they hear Pan piping.

Dorothy M. Weiss
Orlando, FL

Such a Small Thing

"Can you help me?"
This plaintive wail came from a diminutive stranger blocking my way. "Help me," she insisted, "you're taller than me, or you look like you are taller than me, please come with me!" She led me to the cereal section of the huge supermarket. On the top shelf, far beyond her reach was the last box of a cranberry apple cereal she wanted. I stood on tiptoe, stretched high extending my long arms, grasped the box, and gave it to her. She said she had been trying to reach that box, and find a store employee to help her for more than twenty minutes. She saw me, took a chance, and asked for my help. Employees in the store were busy working, restocking supplies aisles away from us and at check-out lines helping other customers. That's why they hadn't responded to her. "You could have been waiting all day," I said. We shook hands, giggling as if we had conquered some formidable marketing foe. She thanked me and we went our separate ways. She was so grateful. Such a small thing, yet she was so appreciative.
I located my half-filled shopping cart two aisles away and continued to the fresh fruits and vegetables section where I almost collided with another shopper as we both reached for the same tomatoes at the same time among a luscious abundant array of vegetables. I stepped back and motioned to this stranger to go ahead. She apologized for being so pushy. I could see she was distraught. "Tough day," I sighed, mumbling to myself. She heard me and started to cry and many of the details of her very pressured harsh hectic life tumbled out as she sobbed that she was so busy with so many responsibilities and duties that she couldn't even get to church, but she believed in God—and she couldn't understand why she was crying because she never allows herself

Dorothy M. Weiss
Orlando, FL

to cry—and she didn't understand why she was babbling to me. I didn't know why either. I was startled and embarrassed but I managed to stammer, "Oh it's okay. I have that effect on people." I searched for tissues in my purse and handed her a wad. She took the tissues, dabbed at her eyes and thanked me. I backed slowly away from her as she began to regain her composure. All I could think of was to give her more space to breathe, "I'm going to the bread department now," I murmured, "but do try to remember that you are strong, your faith, your belief is your source of strength. Slow down a little, if you can, everything will be all right." I don't know why I spoke those words except my mother used to say the same phrase to me whenever I felt overwhelmed and in need of comfort. It worked. The lady managed to give me a weak smile.

I continued on to the bread department, selected my husband's favorite rolls and felt a tug at my elbow. I turned to see one of my neighbors. He looked terrible. He said he had been in a car accident. Words exploded from him. His neck was still in a brace and he was leaning on a cane. He was grateful to be alive. His car was totaled. He said one moment he was driving along just fine. The next thing he knew he was on a stretcher being lifted into an ambulance. He never saw the truck run the red light and slam into him. He couldn't stop talking, with every word he re-lived that awful crash. I just listened to him. Together we selected the bread, rolls, and donuts that we wanted and walked to the pharmacy inside the same supermarket so he could fill his medication prescriptions. I left him there sitting in a chair, talking to other shoppers about his harrowing experience and expressing aloud how fortunate he was to be alive.

Give your best effort every day and leave the rest to Divine Spirit, I remembered reading somewhere. Well today hadn't really been one of my best efforts. I had my own concerns, responsibilities, and a long shopping list. I had started my day somewhat fatigued, dejected, and irritable, but

Dorothy M. Weiss
Orlando, FL

inside the supermarket providing a minor cereal box assist to a stranger, listening briefly to a lady overwhelmed by her problems, and hearing my neighbor describe his frightening, horrific car accident, I stopped feeling sorry for myself. I was truly grateful to be alive and capable of helping others even in such small ways.

As I left the supermarket, I found myself walking with a lighter step and a brighter heart. The sunshine was brilliant. Everything was beautiful once more.

***

Thomas Peter Bennett
Silver Springs, MD

Stormy Evening Ballet

Lightning and thunder
    Transformed the woods
From a darkened stage
    With hidden figures
To a ballet of nature.

Wind and rain choreographed
    Nature's dancing corps.
Maples, ash, oaks, and pines,
    In ageless agile movements,
Tilted, rocked backward,
    Turned, rose, and outstretched
In a thunderous allegro.

First published in *Encore Seasons* by **Goose River Press**, 2017.

Craig Sipe
Orr's Island, ME

Down Tote Road

In the mogul wreckage wake of a Sugarloaf
weekend, careening and flailing over stumps,

I would head back, the Maine-line,
South 27 through drifted shires.

And come the bend into Belgrade Lake
there was a shop sign on the right

that proffered a singular place
they called the Wisdom Center.

And I would slow the truck in passing,
my brood all a snooze around me,

to scoff and guffaw at the New Age Pabulum,
cheer a Sumatra Dark Toast to the flag

then hammer down on my hell bent,
Super-Sized, Big Gulp grind for home.

Today, the store is shuttered
after flirting with a few other shingles,

and I quit skiing five years ago, caved
to broken ribs, and a nose for gravity.

I still go the Loaf for the kids, but no need
to slow on Belgrade Bend anymore.

Even so, as I ponder peeling away
those downhill days from

Craig Sipe
Orr's Island, ME

the Wisdom Center, up creeps a certain
twitch...a secret itch that I might have

Stopped...just...one...time
along the way,

Parked at the Wisdom Center
stepped up to the counter
and ordered a Large.

***

Sandy Conlon
Steamboat Springs, CO

Fly Fisher

She finally did it—
Said the words she vowed to never say—
But there they were in a golden autumn day,
He died doing what he loved.
Fell face first into the stream
With a fish on the end of his hook,
Flailing and flapping in sunlit shallows;
Within the hour it, too, expired
In that solitary place
Caught and released
Man and fish in a moment of grace.

Paul G. Charbonneau
Rockport, ME

Homage to Gustav Holst

Here, planet Earth,
beautiful, troubled Gaia,
a living breathing
suffering presence
wonders, worries and waits.

The Muse rises with Venus,
circles Earth on Mercury's wings
pointing like Bethlehem's star
beyond where Mars bleeds
the color of war,
where Jupiter flexes its muscular pride
and Saturn gathers the circling strains
of time's orbit,
transporting us to the edge, beyond magic,
Neptune!

Muse, what are you doing?
You take us too far...

What of this mystic sphere
where brass breeds softness,
a clarinet's breath beckons inward
while horns lift us beyond thoughts,
stretched between foreboding and hope,
sensing loss and discovery?

Wordless voices yearn and fade,
swoon and fall into a soundless sea,
unfathomable,
where Gaia climaxes and glows
in Neptune's boundless silence.

Stephen Goldfinger
West Newton, MA

Planting Evidence

She showed little knack for solving things in her earliest years. But when she was six Eva surprised her parents by tracing the raccoon droppings to the hole in an ancient oak trunk where their household pests had been living. Not long afterwards she corrected her fifth grade teacher by using a world atlas to prove that Jerusalem was in Asia. Eva also told her that it was the boy with the crooked teeth who had been setting off stink bombs in the closet.

She began to get a bit of a reputation in high school when she discovered that the star pitcher of a visiting baseball team had been doctoring the ball with a tube of vaseline in his back pocket. She was the one who detected a familiar sweet odor wafting from their often spaced-out principal's car when he failed to close its windows. Eva also managed to identify the owner of the knife that slashed the face of the huge bass drum just before the Booster's parade. Her college advisor wrote about this unusual prowess, as well as her considerable academic achievements, when preparing her resume.

At Princeton Eva became a celebrity during the first week's set of rituals when she discovered the rise of jutting bricks that allowed her to climb up to the tower to steal the bell clapper. She linked the bulldog wandering about the gymnasium to the Yalies who had broken in and deflated all the basketballs. And Eva was responsible for the expulsion of two classmates who she found cheating on an exam by using Hershey wrappers laden with minute writing. She also brought down an associate professor when she came upon some revealing emails between him and a sophomore coed.

By then she had acquired the nickname, "Evidence," not too remote from "Eva." It stuck with her throughout her life, and with good reason. After graduation she joined a security

Stephen Goldfinger
West Newton, MA

agency and soon became its most valued investigator. She followed a paper trail to a foreign bank account of a terrorist group. She designed original decryption techniques to trace the collusive deals made by megacorporation CEO's and their surrogates. A clue she obtained from a mistress became the evidence that sent a faith healer from his TV minions to a prison cell. Always hitting upon a minute piece of data, an utterance, a dropped cigar butt and the like to crack the uncrackable.

In a rash bit of pride or temporary insanity she changed her legal surname to the one she had responded to for many years: Evidence.

And so it was that at age 54, true to her instincts, she discovered a quite small irregular black mole that had been missed by her PCP at her regular checkup two months earlier. But by then the black ugly thing had sent little daughter cells throughout her body that set up shop and grew in her liver, lungs, bone and brain. That melanoma, as malignant as they come, killed her within two years.

At her gravesite, as Evidence was being buried, the preacher was droning, "Here she lies in a realm we cannot fathom............" when a single dove descended with a message ribboned to its beak.

"*Friends,*

Don't ask me how but I've found the pearly gates that all others have missed and it's wonderful up here!

Evidence"

Sylvia Little-Sweat
Wingate, NC

Barred Owl at Dark

We sat in darkness, the screen of the porch meshing our darkened
hearts with the black of late September. Hours before we had buried
you, so our talk was quiet and somber even though we made a show
of braving the empty spaces in our souls. You always loved soft
nights on the porch in late summer or early fall, how they gathered our
thoughts like skeins of warmest yarn for the knitting. Now in sorrow,
our hands restive, we wanted to talk you home. An enormous owl,
perched in a nearby tree, broke its instinctive, reclusive way and joined
our talk of you. Its constant song made us somehow aware that you were
there. From deepest human sleep, with the wisdom of the dead,
you also said *It will be all right, it will be all right, it will be all right.*
The owl sang us through the night, our darkest night, with your farewell.

David Campbell
Somerville, MA

Post-Glacial

Is that Orly to O'Hare,
that white stitch westward
across Maine's blue cloth?
A different world. Down here

a pathway shelves a slope,
dips down and turns
among rough-fluted columns
whose needles pave

and tan our course,
where sunny splotches
are stovetop burners
brewing piney spice.

This could be Lake Garda, Como,
these shoreline seethings,
sparks sent flying
off shattered wave tops.

No stolen homeland, human bombs;
but prehistoric daily news
of drumlins, eskers,
pebbles smooth as marbles

high on ridges;
boulders big as trucks
parked anywhere and left idling
for the temporal eternity

David Campbell
Somerville, MA

of thousands of years;
and square miles of terra firma
squashed down to groundwater lodes
by a creeping white plateau,

then primed into lakes
by its disappearance:
all works and gifts
of a glacier's tenure.

***

Julia Rice
Milwaukee, WI

Jack

Jack in black and white,
caught as he speaks a direction,
more alive than a color photo,
he touches a string on his guitar,
his left arm reaching to direct
full sound. Eyes intent, deep
as only a song can express,
the tone within, mouth
beginning to breathe out
devotion, regret, freedom,
the headphones melding all
into a rhythm so rich it rips the soul.

Helen Ackermann
Rothschild, WI

Winter Dreams

It has happened twice now,
the winter which seems
to last forever has
given rise to dreams.

The first was a
challenge to find just the right container
and the right mix of flowers
to place into it.

The second came with a strong desire
to work in the garden, but there was not
a garden space.

What do I fear?
A winter which will never end
or the inability to make gardening a reality.

Surely, there is something!

***

Sally Belenardo
Branford, CT

March

Fifth wheel on axel
of the year, stuck in slushy
rut, with spring in tow.

Janet Morgan
Litchfield, ME

Christmas on the Farm

It was an ideal day to cut a Christmas tree. We didn't have to look for the "perfect" tree, but we could choose one that other people might overlook. After all, I have a history with less than perfect trees. Ever since my father brought home a Charlie Brown tree in revolt of the family's insistence on a tree, any tree, what Christmas trees look like has became secondary to the idea they represent.

This tree only needed to be functional, to serve one purpose. It was to be a tree for the less-than-fussy wild birds that visit our farm during the winter months. Since we were placing it within sight of our kitchen window, even our cats did not complain. When younger, they loved climbing the indoor tree to play with ornaments. Now they are content to sit on our extra wide windowsill and watch all the Christmas tree action going on outside.

So on a snowy day in early December, the tree was soon identified. Ken cut it down, dragged it from the woods, and thrust it into a snow bank directly in line with our kitchen's picture window. Then the fun began: Ken popped the corn and I strung it on thread, alternating the popcorn with raw cranberries. We also looped apple quarters and orange sections on pieces of string to make them look as if they were real ornaments.

As we decorated the tree, I recalled last Christmas. That tree was placed outside only after the wood stove had turned it brown just one day after the gifts had been opened. On that tree when the wild turkeys found the fruit and popcorn, they jumped up and grabbed whole strands of popcorn. Breaking the string, they dragged them off into the woods. The smaller birds had been happy to settle for morsels from the treetop. Eventually the turkeys got the top pieces, too—after they knocked the tree over. Oh, well, watching had been

Janet Morgan
Litchfield, ME

fun—for a while.

This year it was initially the smaller wildlife that received the lion's share of the bounty. They fluttered around, picking off small bits of popcorn. A red squirrel was the first to dash up the tree's trunk and attempt a coup. Bouncing from one limb to another, he initially met with no success. He persisted, however. Going from one apple decoration to another, he tugged and tugged until he finally managed to pull off a whole ornament. We laughed from the warmth of our kitchen as he leapt off into the woods with the section of apple dangling from one corner of his mouth. Before we knew it there were two more apple pieces gone. When we saw the empty loops of string swinging from the branches, I knew it was time to add more apple slices.

The turkeys finally arrived and pecked away at the strings of popcorn and cranberries hanging from the lower branches. They pulled off one piece after another until empty thread was all that remained. One turkey broke a whole strand and as popcorn and cranberries bounced across the snow, she began dashing around and gobbling them up as fast as she could. Her waiting accomplices snatched what remained.

This is the most fun we'd have ever had with a Christmas tree. On Christmas Day we unwrapped our presents just before sunrise. Ken had planned it well, for as the sun rose, my best surprise was soon to be unveiled. When he opened the kitchen curtains, there was my favorite present. Ken had built a 6-foot-tall home entertainment center.

Sitting proudly in the center of the herb garden, my entertainment center was—and still is—the focal point of the yard. A three-foot-long and one-foot wide flat became designated for seeds, raisins, breadcrumbs and cut up apple pieces. On one end was a three-sided set of perches for sitting and eating peanut butter we had pocked into routed holes in the wood; the fourth side was adorned with an orange half. On the opposite end there was a spindle for a

Janet Morgan
Litchfield, ME

dried corncob and a rack for suet. With a roof for protection, it stood just two yards outside our kitchen window. The flat area is at eye level when we sit in front of the window.

My holiday was complete. As we sat at the window with the cats, we wondered what animal would be the first to come to the new feeding station. Ken said it would be a chickadee; I said it would be a pesky red squirrel; I secretly wondered if it would be a blue jay. The chickadee took the day with her inquisitive nature and brave spirit.

***

Margaret Roncone
Vashon, WA

Working Girl in Rose-Red Dress

Tangled
In a slip of a slip
o holy mary
whose prayers go undelivered
whose mind is a pilfered cathedral

o watery rowboat shanty

o holy mary
who strikes the pavement on teetering heels

o holy mary
whose knees bleed from cheap hotel carpets
we humbly pray for you
from the scrubbed floors
of our souls

Laureen Haben, osf
Milwaukee, WI

The Bay of Parables

The sun sparkled on blue-green water
and azure tinted rocks
in a semicircle—
a natural amphitheater.

Standing on a specific hill
across and along
the Sea of Galilee
or sitting in Peter's boat

are the places from which
Jesus chose
to teach parables
about growing:

all around rocky ground
fertile ground
stony ground
even a thorn bush

the story
of the sower
going out
to sow seed.

Parables about seeking:
easily prompted a nod of the head
for the listeners could remember
their experience of a hidden treasure

Laureen Haben, osf
Milwaukee, WI

a pearl of great price
a lost coin
a lost sheep
and maybe a lost son.

And across the water
the rich in Sepphoris and Tiberias
the poor in Capernaum and Nazareth
came to mind:

in the story
of the rich man
and Lazarus
outside the house.

Some were about loving:
the faithful servant
the Good Samaritan
the unforgiving servant

and the friend at night.
No wonder
the Master Teacher
chose this place.

No wonder the listeners
knew where to find Him.

P. C. Moorehead
North Lake, WI

Stone Scrapings

Stone scrapings—
that's my face,
carved from the hills,
cut from slate.

Stone scrapings—
furrowed deep:
water running,
a sob, a weep.

Blossom coming—
bud breaks through.
Sun comes out,
sky so blue.

A smile there,
a tear here.
Stony face,
have no fear.

***

Wing Walker

Wing walker,
wing walker,
fly away home.

Leave your perch
and ride the sky.
Know you're not alone.

Peggy F. Brown
Gray, ME

The Penny Collection

The warm summer breeze gushed through the kitchen window and spread the aroma of bacon and eggs upstairs to Penny's room, causing her to wake in a very pleasant fashion. Penny dressed quickly in her pink seersucker overalls and brushed out her long auburn hair while her belly grumbled with hunger. She took her favorite doll, Nyla, out of her stroller, put a baby bonnet on her golden curls, and carried her down the stairs to the kitchen. She always loved Saturday mornings when her father Everett had time to read the newspaper and stay at home rather than go off to work.

As she reached the bottom step, Penny heard her father say, "Mary, there is an interesting article in today's paper about a boy from Bangor who is the same age as Gerald."

Gerald, Penny's older brother, was somewhere in the South Pacific on a Navy ship. Penny didn't really understand why he had to go away but the grown-ups were very proud of him for doing his "duty for his country," whatever that meant —not something easily understood by eight-year-old Penny. The day Gerald left, he had on a fancy sailor uniform and he carried her around on his shoulders so she could peek into nests to find pretty blue robins' eggs. He wasn't home now and she missed him.

Penny hopped up onto a kitchen chair. As she ate her delicious breakfast, her mother brushed and braided her hair.

Everett continued, "The article explains that young William is stationed in New Mexico with a Mobile Salvage Unit which scours the countryside for scrap metal which is then used to create equipment for the boys fighting overseas. He hopes people will help them by gathering scrap metal in their towns. He wrote his plea in the form of a poem, the first one he ever wrote."

Peggy F. Brown
Gray, ME

Everett cleared his throat, took a deep breath, and eloquently recited this poem:

A Soldier's Plea from Across the Sea
by William J. Clisham

Did you ever live or fight on Bataan, Carregidor or the rest
Of the battlefields where hell and fire rage, and you think of the home that's best,
In America, where love and laughter shine, and freedom lives for all
Of the people whom we left back home, when we heard the Army call?

We all gave up so much you see, so that freedom would always live,
And some of us will never come home, it will be our lives we'll give.
So, for a moment forget your laughter and song, and give a thought for us.
And try hard to give us a helping hand, so that we can end this fuss.

Give us tanks and guns and planes to use, to help us in this strife,
And maybe someday we will be home to live again that happy life.
That piece of junk in your backyard will make a lot of shells;
And guns can be made of that old plow, cultivator or cowbells.

Peggy F. Brown
Gray, ME

*This isn't so much to ask, you see, and I know we
    won't have to beg,*
*Because nobody wants to see us come home, without
    an arm or a leg.*
*Your son's in the foxhole next to us and I know he
    thought of home,*
*Before that bullet parted his hair, that he nevermore
    will comb.*

*So look around your attic, shed or yard and on the
    farm,*
*Your son might live because of you; you found some
    junk in the barn.*
*I know we will be back home now, to listen to those
    freedom bands,*
*Because all of you will help, I know; you won't leave
    us with empty hands.*

"Mary, I feel we should help. We must have some metal we can give up for this cause. It could even help Gerald," stated Everett. "I will ask my customers at work to help; heck everyone knows the boys who have gone off to war and they would be happy to contribute."

Mary quietly wiped a tear from her eye with the edge of her apron. She didn't want Penny to see how much Gerald's absence pained her. It wouldn't be proper to show her emotions in front of her young daughter. She was very proud of Gerald yet sections of that poem gave her vivid images she would like to erase from her mind. She desperately wanted her son to return safe and sound.

Penny thought of Nyla's metal doll stroller. *Would she have to give that up?* She wanted to help Gerald but little Nyla needs her stroller. To busy herself, Penny took Nyla back upstairs to her room and played with her paper doll collection. She could still hear her father's muffled chatter from the kitchen. He continued to chat when the family played

Peggy F. Brown
Gray, ME

checkers and dominoes that afternoon. Later, he went out to speak to townspeople until dinner.

A few days later, Penny and her mother went out for a walk. Nyla was dressed in a gingham dress with a light blanket snuggled around her in the stroller. Penny smiled up at her mother who was dressed in a frilly white blouse and a pretty black and red A-line skirt, which Penny thought looked just like their checkerboard.

As they walked around their neighborhood, Penny noticed that each yard had a pile in the dooryard of discarded metal things. She heard some clanging and noticed Baldy the Blacksmith tossing horseshoes from his shop into a pile. The restaurant across the street had dishpans full of utensils on the front stoop. Penny watched with curiosity as a man who was missing one leg hobbled out of the diner with his crutches and dropped his metal fork in the pan.

Mary saw the wonder in Penny's eyes and said, "I'm so proud of your father for asking all the neighbors and his customers to help gather their scrap metal. The townspeople have collected so much that the Army is sending big trucks next week to pick it all up."

Penny hugged her mother and asked, "Since there is so much already in those piles, can I please keep Nyla's stroller?"

Mary laughed, hugged Penny tight and they returned home with happy hearts knowing Gerald and all the other soldiers would soon hear how much their little town cared.

That evening, Penny looked out her bedroom window and by the light of the gas street lamp, she saw her father adding more scrap metal to the pile in their yard. The light glinted off a horseshoe, almost like it winked at her. "Guess the boy who wrote the poem will be happy to hear this story," she said to Nyla. Penny hopped onto her bed, snuggled Nyla in her arms, closed her eyes and had happy dreams of searching for robins' eggs with her beloved brother Gerald.

Peggy F. Brown
Gray, ME

Author's Note: "A Soldier's Plea from Across the Sea" was written by William J. Clisham of Bangor, Maine while enlisted during WWII. His poem was published in the *Artesia Advocate* (New Mexico) and later reprinted in the *Bangor Daily Commercial* newspaper on July 1, 1943. William J. Clisham was the father of this story's author.

***

Steve Troyanovich
Florence, NJ

the whispers of butterflies...

*Dreamtime...a place of being
outside of us...inside of us*
—John Trudell

like a butterfly's shadow
weeping wings
fatigue a wounded sky
embracing loneliness...
voiceless caresses of time

whispering moments
illusions drift...
eternities stranded
memories dream

grasping tightly
your sheltering smile
sounds of yesterdays
swallow empty tomorrows...

Karen E. Wagner
Ashland, MA

Low Tide

Walking beside the breakers
at low tide, I skip over
the tidal pools like a
child plays hopscotch
with patches of salt water,
momentarily forgetting.

The sea does that
to me,
brings me back
to when the sand crabs
ran between my toes
as I filled my plastic bucket.
These days the wind
has taken its toll on me...
too much time walking
the shore in the sun
until my face takes
on the look of sand
with fine lines etched
around the corners of my mouth,
urchin tracks from the cracks
of my eyes and a brow
with furrowed tidal ridges.
Why can't I be like a
piece of old driftwood,
worn smooth in most places,
valued for its nakedness?

The sea and I are old
friends, we've grown
that way together. When

Karen E. Wagner
Ashland, MA

I was young the sea
was blue. Now that I'm
not so, the sea is grayer
from the storms that kicked it up.
Like me...more
wrinkled, a little grayer and
still playing hopscotch.

***

Julia Rice
Milwaukee, WI

Death Benefits

What was it like?
when you slipped out of life
in the night
and pain poured away
leaving no more bills to pay
no more loneliness.
What is it like
to leave depression
on the nursing home floor
to float into joy
to *know* you are loved
finally to be told
you did more than you could?
Did you grab a handful of happiness
and throw it through the air
taking most of it back with you
but leaving me one crumpled memory?

F. Anthony D'Alessandro
Celebration, FL

Baba's Poon

She rolled around the floor like rigatoni dough in a pasta
 maker's hand.
This seraph seemed escaped from a Rafaello painting three
 rainy seasons past.
Her rippling legs carved by Heaven's lead artist pumped
 and churned.
I reached out, only to be shoved back.
She writhed and wriggled imprisoned by her scarcity of
 words and a pile of pain.
Bullied by this unidentified and anonymous stress, I asked.
"Where does it hurt?"
 Her answer was wrapped in a quiet stare.
I spread out next to her. On the cracked, concrete floor,
an uninvited guest too.
Eye-to-eye, I begged for the magic to inhale her pain.
I paused for a transfer. Nothing happened.
My tiny howler pointed toward her belly button,
defiant tears welling in her eyes.
Minutes later, I slid out of the room, opened a drawer and
 delivered a boxed Swiss spoon to her.
She juggled, fumbled, then ripped the box open, looked up
 at me offering a glacier melting smile.
The crest of the pain eventually retreated and dragged its
 mean spirited curtain away
from this Renaissance child.
At breakfast next sunrise, she demanded, "Baba's 'poon!"

Helen Ackermann
Rothschild, WI

To Be a Savior

A woman from my village and our parish was murdered in a domestic violence confrontation. She was one of four people brutally killed in the shooting spree. I was asked to give a reflection at our parish as part of the memorial prayer held in her honor. Because I recently was typing a memoir about some of my husband's relatives in Germany, I became focused on the concept of savior. The memoir indicated that some of the relatives were members of the Nazi Party with one even being a member of Nazi SS. I wondered why, but in thinking about it even more I realized that with the defeat during World War I and the burdens experienced because of the recession, people in Germany were looking for a savior. It became easier to understand why Adolf Hitler rose to power. He would save Germany, they thought. We have experienced some of the same conditions in our country regarding the need for a savior. People who feel helpless and without power want someone to save them. Perhaps the salvation will come.

In preparing to reflect upon this woman's life, I was struck with the word we use to describe Jesus Christ in our Christian traditions. We use the word Savior. We also believe that in baptism, we put on Jesus Christ. Does this mean we can be saviors too? It seems that we can. The woman of whom I spoke did exactly that in the way she treated the customers in the bank in which she worked. Many recounted how she was able to make them feel better because she paid attention to them and to the stories of their personal lives. She lifted them up from darkness into light. She made them feel whole again. We can all be saviors in our daily lives by our acts of kindness and compassion. That is how the world can truly be saved. It does not depend on only one person who can save us but rather on all of us being able to take our part as saviors in saving one another.

Java L. Collins
Tulsa, OK

A Broken Woman

I am a broken woman
All made up on the outside,
There is no trace of the woman I am to become,
She had vanished, wrapped in a cloud of nothing.
Broken on the inside,
Walking among the shattered pieces of my brokenness.
My sin and shame serving as a filter for the world to see me through.
For nothing can be seen clearly through or by that which is broken.
I cannot see my God with open, blind eyes.
I cannot speak with a voice that arises out of silence.
All that lies before me is
No hope, no future, no faith.
There is no glory in this temple.
I am therefore
Damaged, irreparably broken.
Requiring the permission and acknowledgement of others
To continue to live my life, my dreams.
My human spirit,
So delicate, so sensitive, so damaged...so broken.
Heartbreak, disappointment, misdirection.
Brokenness, it roars when it speaks,
It lies to you in a convincing way,
It steals from you,
And leaves you without a single word of comfort.
My quest to stop living has brought forth death.
So that it now serves as a constant reminder of the pain and suffering,
That are results of my brokenness.
Resisting all attempts of healing,

(continued)

Java L. Collins
Tulsa, OK

Refusing to make His sacrifice count,
Refusing to be forgiven by Him,
Refusing the beauty of His grace and mercy.
Choosing to stay broken.
Look at me,
Look at me,
What do you see?
A broken woman refusing to be free.

***

Mother to Daughter: The Legacy Lives On

In you, I see her strength,
In you, I see her courage,
Her tenacity. Her zest for life,
And the love of her faith!
Mother to daughter, the legacy lives on!
She passed to you a torch that can never be extinguished,
She passed to you lessons that no one else could ever teach
    you.
She gave you love that you did not have to earn,
She gave, so that you could have.
She was there for you always,
Whether in body, soul or spirit.
She shaped you, molded you, trained you,
And did much, much more.
To her, you were perfect.
Mother to daughter, the legacy lives on!
Though she is no longer here physically,
She will always be with you.
Strange as it seems,
Though we try so hard for this not to happen,
We become our mother.

(continued)

Java L. Collins
Tulsa, OK

The truth is,
You were always her, and she you.
In you, I see,
Her beauty, her smile,
I hear her voice, her laughter.
You are the image of her,
A representation of all that she embodied.
Now, you have become all that she is and was and more.
For your children, you are now the mother,
It is your turn to carry the torch, to instill values, faith,
    grace, mercy, love.
For in you, the legacy lives on!

***

Paul G. Charbonneau
Rockport, ME

May Day

I think I saw something
peek through the ground,
though now it seems gone.

A planted perennial perhaps,
or an unwanted weed
posing as a promised flower?

Weed or flower, it will wilt
while I wonder why I wait
for an endless flowering.

Could it be a second sight
spying blossoms everlasting
beyond the final flush of fall?

Joanne Hedou
Rockland, ME

The Colonel

When he spoke, either loudly or quietly, but mostly loudly, words rolled out of his throat as a roar but they were softened by the north woods' wind and humidity and wisdom. You couldn't not listen to him nor could he often stop talking. In the summer in Maine when the temperature was above 90 and the humidity almost 100, he would talk standing and walking. With all the windows open and screened the sound of his voice would be tempered in its travel through the pines but still heard for a long distance. The crickets and peepers would be his chorus although he never knew that.

When he spoke about the help that came to his gentleman-like farm he would usually wave his hand backwards, take a puff on a cigarette or pipe and say, "Mahvelous fellow, just mahvelous." There was no other kind of course, unless, of course, there was and he would say, "I don't know anything about that business. It doesn't sound right to me."

He seemed a typical ex Marine colonel in many ways but when he talked politics and the campaign of George McGovern one realized how much he had lived through. The time in SE Asia was what changed him irrevocably. He could not talk about having been there and he couldn't forget he had either. The drawl, the depression people said he experienced, the condescending way he talked to women as if they were pets—and he often confused them with pets—didn't cover the sad, distanced look he had when he spoke. The things that were a relief: fishing, bird hunting, canoeing—the mainstays of the north woods man—these would take him to a different place.

He had inhabited and roamed in the wild woods of Maine since he was a child. When I knew him, he rarely caught or shot much but the fish were always mahvelous. Bird hunting with him was a quiet walk with a gun and a dog; the gun being silenced so that he could hear and the trigger drawn

Joanne Hedou
Rockland, ME

just a second too late with him lamenting the loss of a pheasant or telling stories of times passed when he had lost many in some conflagration of missteps that were hilarious. The dog received abundant praise for never having been really called on to do its work and that was okay with both him and the dog.

His sons loved and feared him. He was a stranger to the world they had grown up in both literally and figuratively. He had lost them a long time before when he went to fight one war and then he lost them again when he went to fight another; the second time with finality as he also lost his wife to loneliness and abandonment. The story went that he came to town after being in SE Asia looking for the man who had taken her. He didn't find the man and thankfully other men cared for him and brought him back to an acceptable extent from his grief so he lived a long time and saw many grandchildren. He worked in the Congressional Building after his breakdown but that did not change him much. He brought his standard poodle to work with him every day and that is all he ever said about it.

What he could have taught his children and grandchildren if he could have talked more about it; if he had released the pain, given them with love his vision for the world and died knowing that they had received it.

His voice is lost in the woods with the souls of the many dogs he owned in his lifetime. It is whispering to us all. Those he left behind knew how much of what he saw and had lived through was wrong. Let's not repeat those things.

Frank S. Johnson
Greenfield, MO

A Mustering of Courage

Late May finally found its way to the Hoffer house. It was Cindy's birthday. Spiffed up in her favorite flowery dress, she beamed happiness as her friends surrounded her at the kitchen table. The thirteen candles on the white-icing sheet cake waited for her to blow out. From across the kitchen, Mrs. Hoffer smiled as only a proud mother could.

Ready for a birthday soon, too, Cal would turn fifteen in midsummer. He waited with the others for Cindy to make a wish. How tall Cindy was! Her pretty face did not match her gangly height. She was the tallest girl in eighth grade, and he knew how she suffered from the stigma.

***

Cal thought of his mother's words. She had told him a month earlier, "Calvin, Cindy is a long-legged, scrawny puppy now, but just you wait. She will bloom into a drop-dead gorgeous woman in the next few years. Just look at her older sister, Janice. Remember how skinny she was in junior high." With all that said, Mrs. Gibson realized that she had revealed too much, and her face must be flushed red.

"Well, you know what I mean?" Mrs. Gibson finished, turning away and clearly embarrassed by reporting her observations. Her lips formed a hidden but mischievous grin.

"Mom, I just wanted some ideas for her birthday present," Cal said. "You act like I'm going to marry Cindy Hoffer. Cindy's my best friend. You don't marry your best friend."

Cal watched his mom wipe another plate clean from the dinner dishes without answering her only son. Across the drain board Cal peered at his mother in the window glass. Her smile in the reflection said it all. Upset, he stormed out of the kitchen and went to the barn. There at least, he knew his horses wouldn't make fun of him.

Frank S. Johnson
Greenfield, MO

***

Sitting on the front porch steps, Cindy rolled the necklace's small, silver heart between her fingers while she reached her other arm high, waving goodbye. Too soon to her liking, the last of the partygoers had departed. She stared at the cloud of dust springing up behind the car along the gravel road toward Prairiefield. Cal sat beside her, and Cindy was glowing. She liked his present. Cindy heard their parents, now good neighbors as well as good friends, relaxing together in the living room sipping coffee and chatting about the weather and livestock prices. She hoped Cal would kiss her.

The adults were just into their second cup of coffee, when they heard the pack of fierce dogs. Before the men could run to the door, everyone inside heard the explosions, and then the hideous dying yelps and shrieking screams from the only girl they knew to be outside.

By the time the Hoffers and the Gibsons reached the front porch, all was quiet. They saw only Cindy. She stood on the hood of the Gibson's truck sobbing. There was no sign of Cal.

"Where's Cal?" Mr. Gibson hollered looking toward Cindy whose pretty party dress was hiked up to her waist in one hand. He noticed the sheen of the black metal where she stood. The soles of her patent-leather shoes dripped and wetness flowed in a stream to the gravel. He saw that Cindy, near hysteria, could not speak and managed only to point in the direction of the far side of the truck.

Fearfully, Mr. Gibson made his way around his old Ford. There on the ground he saw his son. Mr. Gibson was blubbering like a baby before he reached him. Cal sat in the gravel of the drive in a puddle of blood, his back against the tire. Mr. Gibson saw a blank look on his face. A huge mongrel dog lay over his thigh, coloring his ripped pants with reddened drool. Three other dogs, one larger, sprawled in disarray only a few feet from Calvin. The muscles in their long legs still

Frank S. Johnson
Greenfield, MO

twitched.

Calvin's father reached for the shotgun, now locked in his son's hands. He attempted to pry Cal's fingers away from the wood and metal. "It's okay, son. It's okay. Let me have the gun. I need to finish them. You did good, boy, now let me have the gun." Mr. Gibson finally pulled the bloodied stock away.

The two mothers and Cindy's big sister watched from the porch in shock, but not Mr. Hoffer. He was in a dead run to the truck, all the while over his shoulder watching the pack of wild dogs running in the distance. So many, he thought. So many!

The group on the porch saw Mr. Gibson with the shotgun, and then they saw him reach into the truck and pull out a box of shells. Loading three they saw him with deliberation take two steps and fire down toward the ground, repeat the process two more times, then reload and fire a final shot.

Then, they heard, "You all! I need help! Cal's bleeding badly." Then to Mrs. Hoffer, "Peggy, call the doctor!" To Cindy's dad, "Please, Dale, help me with Cal's leg. I'm not sure I can stop the bleeding." Then, "They were brazen, Dale. They must be rabid."

***

At Prairiefield's medical clinic her party dress now wrinkled and spotted with blood, Cindy again fingered the necklace that hung around her neck. Bringing the silver heart to her tear-moistened lips, her eyes remained locked on her best friend. In her mind she saw the wild dogs attack again. It bewildered her how he had remained so calm, even as the shotgun roared again and again. The last savage dog he had beaten repeatedly with the butt of the gun as its long teeth tore at his leg. *How had he done it? How could anyone?*

Cindy's thoughts were cut short when the nurse politely urged both families to file out into the hallway. Only Cal and

Frank S. Johnson
Greenfield, MO

Cindy's fathers were allowed to stay. The nurse quietly explained how both would be needed to hold Cal down when the boy faced the doctor and the long needle.

"I am not leaving him," Cindy exclaimed.

Everyone looked her way, wondering what to do. Thankfully, the nurse took command. "Is she the girl he saved?" Upon hearing she was, the nurse permitted Cindy to remain on one condition. "Only if you can be calm, child. Can you do that?"

Cindy nodded her head, yes, to the nurse, her eyes on Cal, then to the huge syringe in the doctor's hand, and then back again. She could only think, *Why is it so long?*

While the two parents and Cindy waited, the doctor filled the syringe. Mr. Gibson finally asked his glassy-eyed but conscious son a question he had been holding back since the party. "Cal, why were you two out behind the truck in the first place?" Mr. Gibson quickly realized it was the wrong question at the wrong time and regretted it.

Cindy listened to Mr. Gibson. Her gaze swiftly traveled over to the boy on the bed, then back, and down to the soiled white socks in her dirty new shoes. When Cal didn't say anything the adults looked to her. She also wouldn't answer the question, but she didn't need to. Her blushed face said it all. The two fathers saw the silver heart in her hand, knowing it was her present from Cal.

"I'm sorry, you two," Mr. Gibson blurted out. "That was a stupid question." Another apology came out, and he turned away from the children to his neighbors.

Dale Hoffer's declaration was slow and deliberate, "Your boy saved Cindy's life. Those dogs would have torn her to pieces."

Then Cal's father echoed back in a tearful whisper, "You saved my son."

***

Frank S. Johnson
Greenfield, MO

This slim, resolute girl, just thirteen today was much older this evening than she had been in the afternoon. She held Cal's hand firmly. She watched the doctor inject the first shot of rabies vaccine into his abdomen. Seeing the needle longer than her finger protruding from the syringe nearly made her throw up. As Cal groaned, her hand was crushed by his fingers. Stoically quiet but empathetically clamping her jaw tight, she watched his body arc up and writhe in agony. Only the efforts from her father and Mr. Gibson's strong arms held him.

Cindy bravely bit her lower lip and wouldn't let herself scream. But she hadn't promised the nurse not to cry. Tears streamed down her face. So unimportant she felt right now. Cal was all that mattered.

Slowly, ever so slowly, Cindy watched the muscles in her friend's face relax. His entire body finally lay still. She remembered her father stopping the fountain of blood shooting from Cal's thigh while she watched helplessly from the hood of the truck. She recalled the doctor's words, too. "Mr. Hoffer, you saved the boy's life. You in the war?" Then nodding, "Thought so." Next, with a skeptical tone in his voice Cindy had heard him ask, "And how many wild dogs did the boy kill?"

At that moment as Cindy listened to the physician's words praising her father and Cal, she made herself a promise. Forever more she would listen to any war stories her father felt like telling. He could recite them again-and-again. It didn't matter, even if it was the one she hated most, the one about a beach in a horrible place called Normandy.

Carol Leavitt Altieri
Madison, CT

Driving to Florida Through All Seasons

Starting out, fragile and uncertain.
North winds blowing to scurry the leaves
and stars spreading, leave behind the daylight.
Fortressed in a blue Ford truck (my son called
a hippie one) as hurricane rains pummel.
My friend and I each foresee a different journey.
Two minds, for me an adventure, for him a destination.
I caught my breath as rain and fog spread invisibility.
In the passenger seat engaged in following maps
as we speak, traffic dissects conflicted sentences.
Ken Morr Band plays *Higher Ground*.

Rain in slabs of high tide flow over the truck
and four lanes of traffic interweave.
In some southern states landscapes lie barren
with slivers of tall cypresses and hardwoods
slashed to sparseness.
Hanging moss covers the *hammock* pines
in Carolinas.
Logged forests turn to fields of fog.
My drowsy impression of farmhouses
elicit memories of Flaghill farm
and memories of other journeys with earlier
family. I wonder what he is reflecting on?

Closer to destination, mirrors of intercoastal
water ways ripple
million dollar yachts.
The driver's strong hands on the wheel
we arc across
the Caloosahatchee River.

(continued)

Carol Leavitt Altieri
Madison, CT

And still I see thin, translucent branches
against hazy sky
held fast by twisted trees fading
into taller ones—echoing
the scenery of my childhood farm: orchards,
gardens, pastures, horses and cows.

***

F. Thomas Crowley, Jr
Lincolnville, ME

Every Town...an Island

What if every town was an island?
All shopping done right here
No money being spent away
No corporate takeover fear.

We would have to eat at Donna's
"Coffee, eggs and ham" for you?
No Starbuck latte's sold in town
We're fine with Donna's brew.

You need a car? See Frank in town
At "Smiley's Lot" on Main
I traded in my Jeep (still there)
It only leaks in rain.

The banks would have to go along
And lend us what we need.
We'd pay them back with wages
Earned at "Barney's Grain & Feed."

F. Thomas Crowley, Jr
Lincolnville, ME

Barney's wife works in the store
Where we shop for chicken thighs
From "Tilly's Free Range Chicken Farm"
Not quite Tyson's size.

The money stays on the island friends
There is no place else to spend it.
Besides it all comes back again
To those who spend and lend it.

We'd have to find the leaks for sure
Like buying stuff "on line"
Instead of at the local shops
Like "Mabel's Five and Dime."

I guess it will never happen
But we could make a start
By buying local first instead
And shopping with your heart.

John P. Driscoll
Falmouth, ME

Anger

It was as if I wanted to relive those days, in some way gain a better understanding. Eight days after I got my license and with a fear of suspension bridges, I crossed the Tappan Zee Bridge. I was driving my '57 Chevy Nomad to Nyack, then a small town on the Hudson River. That's where he'd done it three years before. As I drove in a sleeting rain, I thought about him crossing that bridge for the last time, drunk and deeply depressed. It was snowing that day. Normally he would have been in Manhattan working. But in the intervening years I learned that he'd lost his job due to alcoholism. That morning was his to do with as he wanted.

I'd called ahead. The documents would be made available to me as his son. It was difficult finding the coroner's office. Finally, on a slippery, winding road I saw the bunker like building. It was made of cement block like a prison. I got out of the Chevy and began walking to the building with steps which would become the first in the search for a father.

At a control desk in the green tiled reception area I was greeted by a tall, pale, thin man dressed in all white. He had a silver necklace around his neck and introduced himself as Robert Evans, Assistant to the Medical Examiner, Dr. Jonas Cain. Evans said, "We've been expecting you. May I see your ID?" He studied it, "Well, Mr. Egan, follow me."

He led me into a room with no windows. The room was cool and filled with metal files. He went to a file cabinet and pulled a folder. Then he sat me at a wooden table that had one lamp, saying, "Linus, if you have any questions come out and get me."

I thanked him and opened my father's folder. I first went to the back of the pages and found the summary statement. I read it closely...

John P. Driscoll
Falmouth, ME

The deceased was found in the orchard off Meadow Lane. The snow was heavy, temperature approximately thirty. The body was found sitting against a tree. The body was covered in snow. The snow on the left side of the head was bloody. The legs were crossed and the arms were at the sides of the body. A .22 caliber Smith and Wesson revolver lay beyond the left hand. Urine was noted in the snow covering the pelvis. Rigor Mortis was present.

At post mortem rigor mortis was profound. A reticular pattern was noted on the skin throughout. The eyes were open. A 2 cm entry wound was noted in the left temple. Exit occurred behind the right ear. There was little disfigurement. The cortex of the brain was lacerated with shredding noted at the margins. The other findings of note were benign hypertrophy of the prostate and chronic, advanced cirrhosis of the liver.

It was signed Jonas Cain, MD, and dated February 21, 1963.

I closed the folder, left it on the table and walked out to the central desk where Evans sat talking to a short man in an overcoat, hat and gloves. When they finished talking, I went to Evans and thanked him. Then I asked him directions to the orchard off Meadow Lane. Once in the car, I sat, chewed a piece of gum and thought how my father had been reduced to clinical words on a page. There was nothing left of him after cremation. There was no grave or remembrance where I lived with a younger brother and a mother prone to delusion. There had been no will, no legacy.

In a heavier snow I found Meadow Lane. The orchard was to the right behind a mossy stone wall. There was a white canopy from the trees and a smell of wood smoke from a house in the distance. I walked over the wall into the orchard. All sound was muffled by the snow. I felt lonely. Yes, it was a lonely place to die. I wondered what tree. But

John P. Driscoll
Falmouth, ME

this was lost in the silent history and mystery that had become my father.

The trip back over the bridge was slick and slow but the Nomad held the road. When I arrived home dinner had been served. My mother was angry that I was late. She wanted to know where I'd been. I mentioned nothing of Nyack. The reason I was seeking facts was because my mother at first would not and then could not provide them. Even then I recognized that her understanding of that day had become tangled by her imagination as it attempted to assuage her guilt through fantasy. I believed that her fantasy began the night of the death when she arranged for her lover, a middle aged developer, to tell my brother and me of our father's death. In an upstairs bedroom he said simply, "Your father is dead."

I looked at him as he spoke those words. I felt angry at him and treacherously abandoned by my father. I knew it was suicide, the word the man was ashamed to say. I felt him weak and an intruder.

That unsaid word had been indelibly imprinted on my thoughts by a conversation the night before. Over drinks my father had used the word several times in talking to my mother as they sat before a fire in the living room. We had been put to bed. I listened from the stairs. I returned to bed wondering whether I should tell him I loved him. *Would it do any good*, I questioned? I said nothing. I have only recently recognized the word and the emotion that prevented me from speaking—embarrassment. I felt I didn't know my father well enough to use the word love and it didn't seem masculine to a thirteen year old boy.

With those thoughts I went to school the next day. My birthday had been Saturday the 16th of February. My father died on Wednesday the 20th at approximately 1:30 p.m. according to the documents in Nyack. That day I was at school at 7 a.m. I had classes until 1 p.m. Then I went to wrestling practice. I was training for a match with Richie Simms, the heavy weight champion the year before. I was

John P. Driscoll
Falmouth, ME

undefeated. We were matched for the title of Heavyweight Champion of Westchester County, 13-15 years. The match was scheduled for Saturday, February 23rd. Practice was hard. I had to lose weight in a rubber suit. At the end I was exhausted. I showered and with three friends walked to town where it was my father's turn to pick us up.

It wasn't his car that pulled up. It was the developer's car. She had sent him to pick us up. Before I got into the backseat I felt it. I knew my father was dead. From what I'd heard the night before I thought suicide. I didn't want any of my friends to hear me cry so I said nothing. I said nothing to the developer when he stopped at my house. I got out and walked down the walk to the front door. The developer walked behind me. I opened the door and went directly to the kitchen. My mother was sitting at the kitchen table. She had a drink. She wasn't crying. With red eyes she looked past me to the kitchen doorway. I turned. The developer was standing there. My mother said, "Linus, please go upstairs; your brother is already there. Please go up now."

"Where's Dad?"

"Linus, please go with Jim."

I felt his hand on my shoulder. He turned me toward the stairs. I remember a tide of rage but then it left, quickly replaced by a placid dream state where nothing seemed real, not the room, my brother, Jim or his words when he told us. My brother cried. He seemed smaller to me. For an instant I thought he was made of glass. I was in the nightmare of abandonment. I was in some way worthless, unworthy of my father's love.

I went to bed wondering who would now pickup the babysitter, who'd go for cigarettes at night, who'd carve the turkey? I wondered who'd take me to the Harvard Princeton game, who'd be in the stands on Saturday? I fell asleep with these questions. I slept until sunrise when I sensed other people in the house. In my pajamas I went downstairs. Sitting in the kitchen were my grandparents. Overnight they

John P. Driscoll
Falmouth, ME

had driven from Boston. They stood and came to me together. They hugged me. My grandmother got me a glass of orange juice and we sat at the kitchen table. They said some things but never used the words death or suicide. I sensed they forbid themselves the word suicide. They were Catholic. It was as if the family had sinned, was shamed. They acted guilty of something. I didn't feel like I had done anything to be ashamed or guilty of. I felt disgruntled and sad. I sat on a radiator cover and alone read *Cry, the Beloved Country*.

During the day a few people came with food. Some of my parent's friends didn't come to our house. I noticed this. I felt their absence and the absence of their children, my friends. I began thinking perhaps it was all dirty, sinful, shameful. I mean what he'd done.

Unknown to me my wrestling coach called my mother that day. He explained how hard I'd trained for the match with Simms. He promised to keep me under his wing if she would allow me to wrestle on Saturday. She consented.

Friday I went to wrestling practice in the afternoon. A couple of the guys said they were sorry. No one said anything more. I had a hard time keeping my mind on Simms and Saturday.

After practice Coach McLaren called me to his office. He was sweating. So was I. The room smelled of Bengay. Papers and rolls of tape were on the desk. There was one telephone on the desk and no windows. Coach was sitting at the desk. He stood up. He was tall with a blonde crew cut and deeply cut jaw. He put his hands on my shoulders and bent to look directly into my eyes. It was the first kind gesture that I'd felt in a week. This kindness caused tears to stream down my cheeks. The coach put his arms around me and hugged me. I could smell his aftershave. After he held me he let me go and we both sat. It was then that I knew someone understood my isolation, that someone could feel my pain and sense the dark shame that I carried. "Linus," he said.

John P. Driscoll
Falmouth, ME

"Are you okay, son?"

"Yes."

"In your heart Linus what do you want to do about tomorrow?"

"I want to wrestle, Coach."

"Are you feeling sadness?"

"No. I'm angry, Coach."

"About what?"

"About feeling guilty without having done anything. The only thing I didn't do was to tell him I loved him. Did that make a difference, Coach?"

"No, Linus. You're right you haven't done anything wrong, son. People are afraid of what happened to your father. It makes them think about their own deaths and that scares them.

"Many people don't know what to say. So they say nothing and you feel they don't care. They're just scared Linus. Do you understand what I'm saying?"

"Yes, Coach."

"The anger you feel, Linus, will hurt you on Saturday. It stiffens the muscles and affects judgment so that the match becomes a fight. Maybe we should let you sit this one out."

"No, Coach. Please. I want to wrestle."

"Well then, all right, but anytime you want to withdraw, Linus, let me know. It'll be okay, son. Now get yourself home and be with your family."

"Yes, Coach."

That evening Wayne's father picked us up. Everyone in the car knew. There was no conversation, none of the usual joking and kidding around. I felt alone. Everything was out of place and distorted. I was anxious about Saturday.

When I got home my mother told me that a small service for my father was held that morning. She hadn't wanted me or my brother to go. Again I felt angry. It was like he disappeared on me in some macabre game of hide and seek. Now she was telling me that he was gone with no trace.

John P. Driscoll
Falmouth, ME

I said nothing at dinner. The others were whispering as if they were hiding from something, or in some way guilty. Did I look like them? *Was I hiding from admitting that he was gone? Was I guilty like them because I never told him I loved him?* I wondered about these things while moving the food around my plate with a knife and fork. My grandfather carved. My grandmother then excused me from the table.

I went to my bedroom to read some more of the book and to be alone. I put my head on the pillow. I dreamt. I remember running after the developer. I was chasing him as if he had gotten away with something, perhaps taking something of mine. As I ran, he disappeared. Then everything disappeared into a long night of an irritable sleep.

When I awoke no one was up. The house was hushed of its whispers. I had a glass of orange juice. I couldn't eat until I'd weighed in for the match. At seven Coach picked me up. We had to be at the Rye Gym before 9 a.m. When I got in Coach said, "Good morning, Linus."

"Coach."

"Ready to go, son?"

"Yes."

We didn't talk for awhile. He was listening to Gilbert and Sullivan on the radio. The music and the words made me smile for the first time in days. Coach kept his eyes on the road. Then he asked, "Still angry, Linus?"

"Yes, Coach."

"Remember our conversation yesterday. You're not in there to fight Simms. You're there to influence him into making a mistake that you can take advantage of. You can't influence him using anger. He'll simply out muscle you. Do you understand, Linus?"

"Yes."

"I think you can win this thing, Linus, but you've got to establish and maintain a calmness. Anger will only take that calmness away. Then you've given up your strongest muscle and that's you ability to think your way through a match.

John P. Driscoll
Falmouth, ME

That's how you've gotten here, Linus. You've lost enough, Linus. Don't lose this. Okay, son?"

"Yes, Coach."

We drove on listening to the music. *How could I stop or hold back such a strong feeling of abandonment and its anger?* I concentrated on the music. It calmed me. I thought how wonderful it was that two people like Gilbert and Sullivan could work so closely. They were coordinated, each taking advantage of the other's skills. I had to figure out Simms's skills and work with them to beat him. By far his greatest skill was the use of his raw strength. I had to let him think he was winning to take advantage of him. It would be turning his strength against him. Coach drove silently also listening to the music. I felt my anger weakening.

In the locker room I stripped to my underwear. The officials weighed me in. I made the 180 pound limit by two pounds. Coach gave me some oranges to eat. I never saw Simms until the match.

When I did see him he was taller than me, more heavily muscled. His black skin looked blue in the lights. We started on our feet. His hand felt hard on my neck. Twice he threw me to the mat to earn points. The second time he pinned my arms in back of me. He was trying to roll me on my back when the first period ended. I tried to keep Coach's words in my mind. It was a matter of using my strength with his, not angrily against him.

I started the second period in the down position. He immediately tied up my legs. I couldn't stand. I looked to Coach, he was screaming something to me but I couldn't hear him. The crowd noise had sealed me into an envelope where I was alone again. My mind tumbled. My muscles ached under the strain of Simms' strength. My face was being burned by the mat. Suddenly Simms rolled to the right with his hips. Instead of resisting him I rolled with him. He over estimated my resistance and rolled onto his back. I was on top. I put one of his arms behind my neck and leaned into

                                                    John P. Driscoll
                                                    Falmouth, ME

his chest. I looked up at the stands. I saw them screaming. They were stomping their feet for a pin. What I didn't see was my father. With all the anger in me I stretched Simms' arm further back putting both of his shoulders on the mat. The referee pounded the mat with his palm. The whistle blew. Simms let out a groan under me. We stood and the short referee raised my hand. Later they gave Simms the silver medal and me the gold. On that medal where my father's name was to have been engraved I had Coach's name put on.

***

Fifty years later there was an occasion in my home town. The new high school gym was dedicated to and named after Coach. I was asked to speak. I traveled down from Maine. I spoke, telling this story. After my words I gave Coach that gold medal. Later I crossed the Hudson on the bridge that I never trusted. I went to Nyack and then to the orchard off Meadow Lane. I sat with my back against a tree. I've never lost my anger.

Christopher Fahy
Thomaston, ME

Second Thoughts

Repairing the hole in the floor
of the open chamber,
that unfinished upstairs room
at the end of the ancient wreck he bought,
the wood of its walls and slanted ceiling
black with age and smelling of sour dust,
he feels the heavy past of everyone
who ever lived there, feels the weight
of all the work still left to do
with winter coming on
and wonders if he's made a huge mistake.

The narrow space has just one source
of light, where he removed
the shattered window.
He turns to that brilliant portal
framing the soft September afternoon—
the shining field, the distant evergreens,
pure cobalt sky—and rides the steady rasp
of autumn crickets, freed by this golden moment
from his thoughts of cold and dark.

GOOSE RIVER ANTHOLOGY, 2018

We seek selections of fine poetry, essays, and short stories (3,000 words or less) for the 16th annual *Goose River Anthology, 2018*. The book will be beautifully produced with full color cover and full color dust jacket for hard covers.

You may submit even if you have been published before in a previous edition of the *Goose River Anthology*. We retain one-time publishing rights. All rights revert back to the author after publication. You may submit as many pieces as you like.

EARN CASH ROYALTIES. Author will receive a 10% royalty on all sales that he or she generates.

There is no purchase required and nothing is required of the author for publication. Deadline for submissions is April 30, 2018. Publication will be in the fall of 2018 (they make great Christmas gifts). Guidelines are as follows:

- Submit clean, typed copy by snail mail—**mandatory**
- Email a Word or rtf file to us (if possible)
- Reading fee: $1.00 per page
- Do not put two poems on the same page
- Essays and short stories must be double-spaced
- **SASE (#10 or larger) for notification** (one forever stamp) plus additional postage for possible return of submission if desired.
- Author's name & address at top of each page of paper copy and first page of emailed copies.

Submit to:
Goose River Anthology, 2018
3400 Friendship Road
Waldoboro, ME 04572-6337
E mail: gooseriverpress@roadrunner.com
www.gooseriverpress.com